The Scientific Method

Arrange the steps of the scientific method in the proper order.

_____   Research the problem.

_____   Observe and record.

_____   Make a hypothesis.

_____   Identify the problem.

_____   Arrive at a conclusion.

_____   Test the hypothesis.

Match each term with the correct definition.

_____   1.   hypothesis

_____   2.   control

_____   3.   variable

_____   4.   experiment

_____   5.   conclusion

_____   6.   theory

_____   7.   data

A. organized process used to test a hypothesis

B. an educated guess about the solution to a problem

C. observations and measurements recorded during an experiment

D. a judgment based on the results of an experiment

E. a logical explanation for events that occur in nature

F. used to show that the result of an experiment is really due to the condition being tested

G. factor that changes in an experiment

Safety in the Laboratory

Identify what is wrong in each laboratory situation.

1.

_____
_____
_____

2.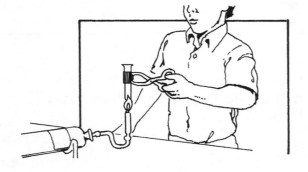

_____
_____
_____

3.

_____
_____
_____

4.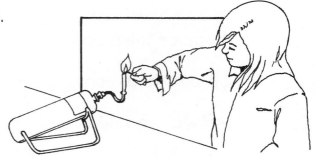

_____
_____
_____

5.

_____
_____
_____

6.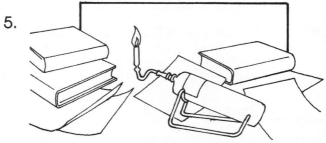

_____
_____
_____

Laboratory Equipment

Write the name of each lab instrument or piece of equipment.

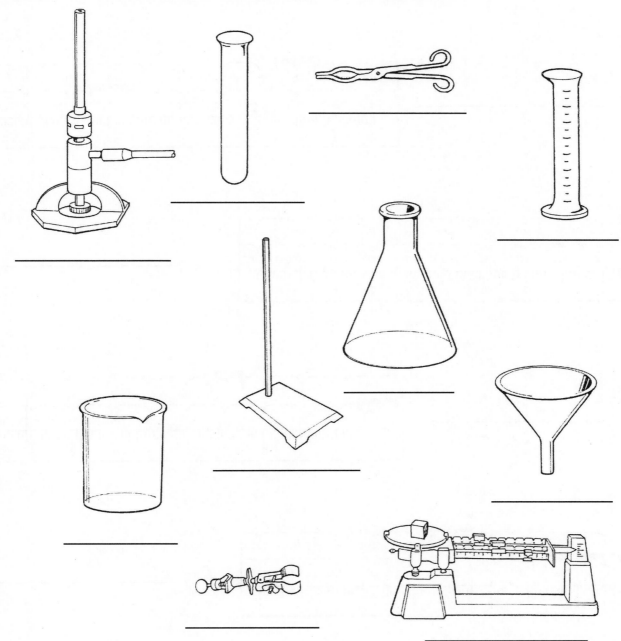

_____

balance   beaker   Bunsen burner
Erlenmeyer flask   funnel   graduated cylinder
ring stand   test tube   test tube clamp
tongs

Using the Balance

Identify the mass shown on each balance.

_____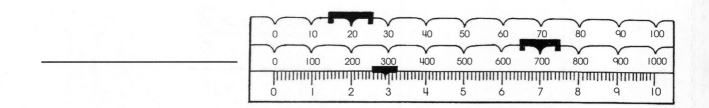

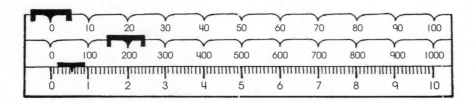 _____

_____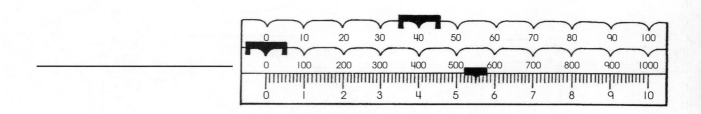

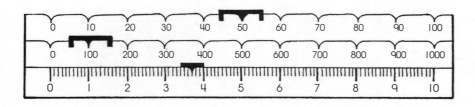 _____

_____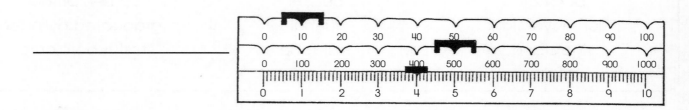

Measuring Length

Identify the lengths marked on the centimeter ruler.

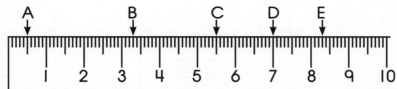

	cm	**mm**
A.	_____	_____
B.	_____	_____
C.	_____	_____
D.	_____	_____
E.	_____	_____

Measure each line with a centimeter ruler.

1. _____

2. _____

3. _____

4. _____

5. _____

6. _____

7. _____

Measuring Liquids

Identify the volume indicated on each graduated cylinder. The unit of volume is mL.

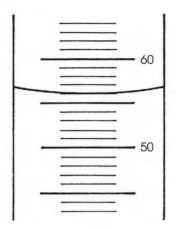
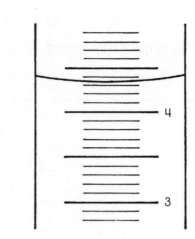
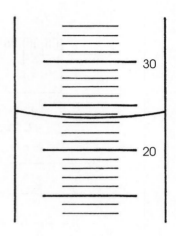

1. _____   4. _____   7. _____

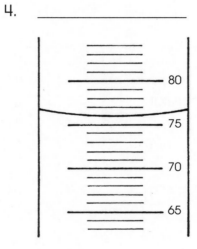
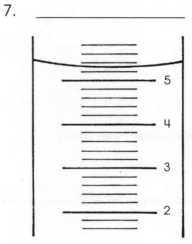

2. _____   5. _____   8. _____

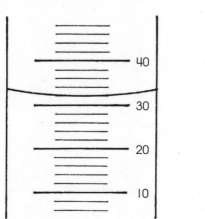
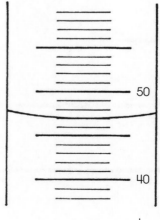

3. _____   6. _____   9. _____

Reading Thermometers

Identify the temperature indicated on each thermometer. The unit is °C.

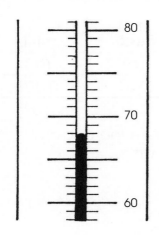

1. _____

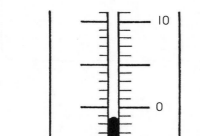

2. _____

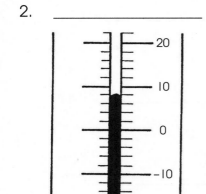

3. _____

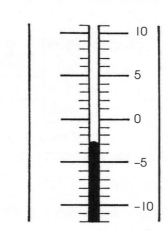

4. _____

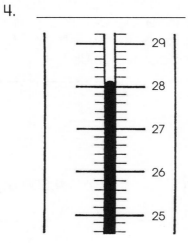

5. _____

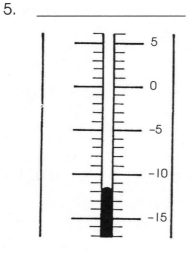

6. _____

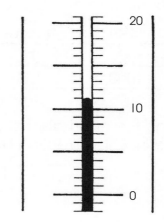

7. _____

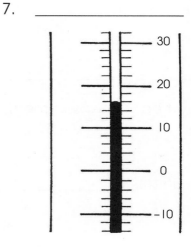

8. _____

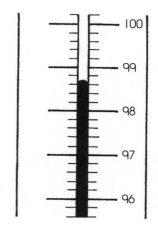

9. _____

Metrics and Measurement

Scientists use the metric system of measurement, which is based on the number 10. It is important to be able to convert from one unit to another.

kilo-	hecto-	deca-	Basic Units	deci-	centi-	milli-
(k)	(h)	(da)	gram (g)	(d)	(c)	(m)
1000	100	10	liter (L)	0.1	0.01	0.001
10^3	10^2	10^1	meter (m)	10^{-1}	10^{-2}	10^{-3}

Using the chart above, we can determine how many places to move the decimal point and in what direction by counting the places from one unit to the other.

Example: Convert 5 mL to L.

Answer: To go from milli (m) to the basic unit (liters), count on the above chart three places to the left. Move the decimal point three places to the left and 5 mL becomes 0.005 L.

Convert each measurement.

1. 35 mL = _____ dL

2. 950 g = _____ kg

3. 275 mm = _____ cm

4. 1.0 L = _____ kL

5. 1.0 mL = _____ L

6. 4,500 mg = _____ g

7. 25 cm = _____ mm

8. 0.005 kg = _____ dag

9. 0.075 m = _____ cm

10. 15 g = _____ mg

Unit Conversions and Factor-Label Method

Another method of converting from one unit to another involves multiplying by a conversion factor. A **conversion factor** is a fraction that is equal to one. For example, 60 minutes is equal to 1 hour. Therefore, 60 min./1 hr. or 1 hr./60 min. = 1. When you multiply by the number 1, the value of the number is not changed, although the units may be different.

Example: How many milligrams are in 20 kilograms?

Use the following relationships:

1,000 mg = 1 g

1,000 g = 1 kg

1. Start with the original number and unit.
2. Multiply by a unit factor with the unit to be discarded on the bottom and the desired unit on top.
3. Cancel units.
4. Perform numerical calculations.

$$20 \text{ kg} \times \frac{1000 \text{ g}}{1 \text{ kg}} \times \frac{1000 \text{ mg}}{1 \text{ g}} = 20{,}000{,}000 \text{ or } 2 \times 10^7 \text{ mg}$$

Perform each conversion using unit factoring.

1. 500 mL = _____ L

2. 25 cg = _____ g

3. 400 mg = _____ kg

4. 30 cm = _____ mm

5. 3500 sec. = _____ hr.

6. 1.25 L = _____ mL

7. 15 m = _____ mm

8. 0.75 L = _____ mL

9. 6.4 kg = _____ g

10. 7,200 m = _____ km

11. 4.2 L = _____ mL

12. 0.35 km = _____ m

13. 2.3 L = _____ mL

14. 4.5 yd. = _____ in.

15. 50 mm = _____ km

16. 150 mg = _____ g

17. 150 kg = _____ g

18. 23 mL = _____ L

19. 0.156 g = _____ mg

20. 2 yr. = _____ sec.
    (Assume 1 year = 365 days)

Using Correct Units

For each of the following commonly used metric measurements, identify its symbol. Then, use the symbols to complete each sentence.

_____ milliliter   _____ milligram   _____ liter   _____ centimeter

_____ kilogram   _____ millimeter   _____ kilometer   _____ gram

_____ meter   _____ millisecond   _____ microgram   _____ nanometer

1. Colas may be purchased in one- or two-_____ bottles.

2. The mass of a bowling ball is 7.25 _____.

3. The length of the common housefly is about 1 _____.

4. The mass of a paper clip is about 1 _____.

5. One teaspoon of cough syrup has a volume of 5 _____.

6. The speed limit on the highway is usually 106.6 _____/h or 29.6 _____/s.

7. The length of the small intestine in a man is about 6.25 _____.

8. Viruses such as AIDS, polio, and flu range in length from 17 to 1,000 _____.

9. Adults require at least 1,000 _____ of calcium to meet the US RDA.

10. In a vacuum, light can travel 300 km in 1 _____.

11. The mass of a proton is 1.67×10^{-18} _____.

12. Blue light has a wavelength of about 500 _____.

13. One mole of oxygen gas at STP occupies 22.4 _____.

14. Myoglobin, a protein that stores oxygen, has a mass of 2.98×10^{-14} _____ .

15. Buttery popcorn contained in a large 1-_____ bowl has a mass of about 50 _____ of fat and about 650 calories.

16. The dying comet fragments that continue to batter Jupiter travel at speeds of about 58,117 _____ /_____, or 130,000 miles per hour.

17. The human heart has a mass of about 1.05 _____.

18. Stand with your arms raised out to your side. The distance from your nose to your outstretched middle finger is about 1 _____.

19. The body mass of a flea is about 0.5 _____, and it can jump about 20 _____ high.

20. On a statistical basis, smoking a single cigarette lowers your life expectancy by 642,000 _____, or 10.7 minutes.

Scientific Notation

Scientists very often deal with very small and very large numbers, which can lead to a lot of confusion when counting zeros. We can express these numbers as powers of 10 so they are easier to read and understand.

Scientific notation takes the form of $M \times 10^n$ where $1 \leq M <$ and n represents the number of decimal places to be moved. Positive n indicates the standard form is larger than zero, whereas negative n would indicate a number smaller than zero.

Example: Convert 1,500,000 to scientific notation.

Move the decimal point so that there is only one digit to its left, a total of 6 places.

$$1,500,000 = 1.5 \times 10^6$$

Example: Convert 0.00025 to scientific notation.

Move the decimal point 4 places to the right.

$$0.00025 = 2.5 \times 10^{-4}$$

(Note that when a number starts out less than one, the exponent is always negative.)

Convert each number to scientific notation.

1. 0.005 = _____

2. 5,050 = _____

3. 0.0008 = _____

4. 1,000 = _____

5. 1,000,000 = _____

6. 0.25 = _____

7. 0.025 = _____

8. 0.0025 = _____

9. 500 = _____

10. 5,000 = _____

Convert each number to standard notation.

11. 1.5×10^3 = _____

12. 1.5×10^{-3} = _____

13. 3.75×10^{-2} = _____

14. 3.75×10^2 = _____

15. 2.2×10^5 = _____

16. 3.35×10^{-1} = _____

17. 1.2×10^{-4} = _____

18. 1×10^4 = _____

19. 1×10^{-1} = _____

20. 4×10^0 = _____

Calculations Using Significant Figures

When multiplying numbers in scientific notation, multiply the first part of the number, the **mantissa**, and add the exponents.

Example: $(3.0 \times 10^2)(2.5 \times 10^6) =$

Multiply: $3.0 \times 2.5 = 7.5$

Then, add: $2 + 6 = 8$

$= 7.5 \times 10^8$

When dividing numbers in scientific notation, divide the mantissa and subtract the exponents.

Example: $\dfrac{9.0 \times 10^6}{4.5 \times 10^2}$

Divide: 9.0 by $4.5 = 2.0$

Then, subtract: $2 - 6 = 4$

$= 2.0 \times 10^4$

Perform each calculation. Express all answers in scientific notation.

1. $(1.5 \times 10^3)(3.5 \times 10^5)$	6. $(4 \times 10^5) \div (1 \times 10^{-3})$
2. $(2.0 \times 10^8)(2.0 \times 10^6)$	7. $(7.6 \times 10^{-3})(8.2 \times 10^{-4})$
3. $(6.2 \times 10^6) \div (3.1 \times 10^2)$	8. $(8.5 \times 10^{-8}) \div (2.5 \times 10^{-3})$
4. $(5.0 \times 10^4) \div (2.5 \times 10^3)$	9. $(7.0 \times 10^{11})(7.0 \times 10^{-11})$
5. $(6.8 \times 10^7)(2.2 \times 10^{-5})$	10. $(1.3 \times 10^{-5}) \div (2.6 \times 10^{-9})$

Name_____

Density

Which has the greater mass, air or lead? Most would answer lead, but this question actually does not have an answer. To compare these two things, you need to know how much of each you have. A large amount of air could have a greater mass than a small amount of lead. To compare different things, we have to compare the masses of each that occupy the same space, or volume. This is called **density**. It is measured in units of g/mL or g/cm^3.

$$\text{density} = \frac{\text{mass}}{\text{volume}} \quad \text{or} \quad D = \frac{M}{V}$$

Solve each problem.

1.	What is the density of carbon dioxide gas if 0.196 g occupies a volume of 100 mL?
2.	A block of wood that measures 3.0 cm on each side has a mass of 27 g. What is the density of the block?
3.	An irregularly shaped stone was lowered into a graduated cylinder holding a volume of water equal to 2.0 mL. The height of the water rose to 7.0 mL. If the mass of the stone was 25 g, what was its density?
4.	A 10.0 cm^3 sample of copper has a mass of 89.6 g. What is the density of copper?
5.	Silver has a density of 10.5 g/cm^3, and gold has a density of 19.3 g/cm^3. Which would have a greater mass, 5 cm^3 of silver or 5 cm^3 of gold?
6.	Five mL of ethanol has a mass of 3.9 g , and 5.0 mL of benzene has a mass of 4.4 g. Which liquid is denser?
7.	A sample of iron in the shape of a rectangular prism has the dimensions of 2 cm × 3 cm × 2 cm. If the mass of this object is 94 g, what is the density of iron?

13

Graphing of Data

Graphing is an important tool in science. It enables us to see trends that are not always obvious. Graph the following data and answer the questions below.

Mass of Liquid (g)	Volume of Liquid (cm³)
20	4
100	20
75	15
40	8
10	2

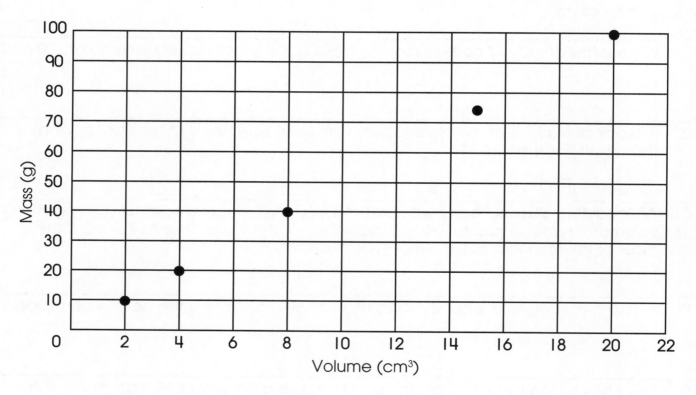

1. As mass increases, what happens to the volume? _____

2. As volume increases, what happens to the mass? _____

3. How many grams of liquid would occupy 12 mL? _____

4. What volume would 90 g of liquid occupy? _____

5. What is the density of the liquid? _____

Name_____

Determining Speed (Velocity)

Speed is a measure of how fast an object is moving or traveling. **Velocity** is a measure of how fast an object is traveling in a certain direction. Both speed and velocity include the distance traveled compared to the amount of time taken to cover this distance.

$$speed = \frac{distance}{time}$$ $$velocity = \frac{distance}{time} \text{ in a specific direction}$$

Solve each problem.

1. What is the velocity of a car that traveled a total of 75 kilometers north in 1.5 hours? _____

2. What is the velocity of a plane that traveled 3,000 miles from New York to California in 5.0 hours? _____

3. John took 45 minutes to bicycle to his grandmother's house, a total of four kilometers. What was his velocity in km/h? _____

4. It took 3.5 hours for a train to travel the distance between two cities at a velocity of 120 miles/h. How many miles lie between the two cities? _____

5. How long would it take for a car to travel a distance of 200 kilometers if it is traveling at a velocity of 55 km/h? _____

6. A car is traveling at 100 km/h. How many hours will it take to cover a distance of 750 km? _____

7. A plane traveled for about 2.5 hours at a velocity of 1,200 km/h. What distance did it travel? _____

8. A girl is pedaling her bicycle at a velocity of 0.10 km/min. How far will she travel in two hours? _____

9. An ant carries food at a speed of 1 cm/s. How long will it take the ant to carry a cookie crumb from the kitchen table to the ant hill, a distance of 50 m? Express your answer in seconds, minutes, and hours. _____

10. The water in the Buffalo River flows at an average speed of 5 km/h. If you and a friend decide to canoe 16 kilometers down the river, how many hours and minutes will it take? _____

Name_____

Calculating Average Speed

Graph the following data and answer the questions below.

Time (min.)	Distance (m)
0	0
1	50
2	75
3	90
4	110
5	125

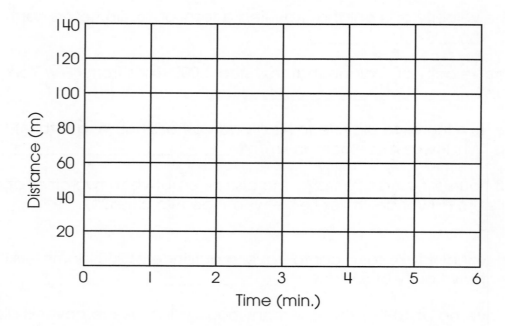

average speed = $\dfrac{\text{total distance}}{\text{total time}}$

1. What is the average speed after two minutes? _____

2. What is the average speed after three minutes? _____

3. What is the average speed after five minutes? _____

4. What is the average speed between two and four minutes? _____

5. What is the average speed between four and five minutes? _____

Acceleration Calculations

Acceleration means a change in speed or direction. It can also be defined as a change in velocity per unit of time. It is measured in units such as km/h/s and m/s/s (m/s^2).

$$a = \frac{v_f - v_i}{t}$$

where a = acceleration
v_f = final velocity
v_i = initial velocity
t = time

Calculate the acceleration for the following data.

	Initial Velocity	Final Velocity	Time	Acceleration
1.	0 km/h	24 km/h	3 s	_____
2.	0 m/s	35 m/s	5 s	_____
3.	20 km/h	60 km/h	10 s	_____
4.	50 m/s	150 m/s	5 s	_____
5.	25 km/h	1,200 km/h	2 min.	_____

6. A car accelerates from a standstill to 60 km/h in 10.0 seconds.

   What is its acceleration? _____

7. A car accelerates from 25 km/h to 55 km/h in 30 seconds.

   What is its acceleration? _____

8. A train is accelerating at a rate of 2.0 km/h/s. Its initial velocity is 20 km/h.

   What is its velocity after 30 seconds? _____

9. A runner achieves a velocity of 11.1 m/s 9 seconds after he begins.

   What is his acceleration? _____

Name_____

Graphing Speed vs. Time

Graph the following data and answer the questions below.

Speed (km/h)	Time (s)
0.0	0
10.0	2
20.0	4
30.0	6
40.0	8
50.0	10

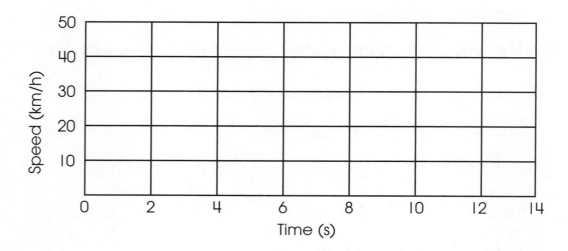

1. As time increases, what happens to the speed? _____

2. What is the speed at 5 s? _____

3. Assuming constant acceleration, what would be the speed at 14 s? _____

4. At what time would the object reach a speed of 45 km/h? _____

5. What is the object's acceleration? _____

6. What would the shape of the graph be if a speed of 50.0 km/h is maintained from 10 s to 20 s? _____

7. Based on the information in problem 6, calculate the acceleration from 10 s to 20 s.

   _____

8. What would the shape of the graph be if the speed of the object decreased from 50.0 km/h at 20 s to 30 km/h at 40 s? _____

9. What is the acceleration in problem 8? _____

Graphing Distance vs. Time

Graph the following data and answer the questions below.

Distance (km)	Time (s)
0	0
5	10
12	20
20	30
30	40
42	50
56	60

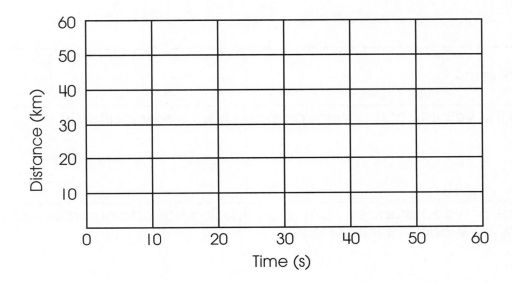

1. What is the average speed at 20 s? _____

2. What is the average speed at 30 s? _____

3. What is the acceleration between 20 s and 30 s? _____

4. What is the average speed at 40 s? _____

5. What is the average speed at 60 s? _____

6. What is the acceleration between 40 s and 60 s? _____

7. Is the object accelerating at a constant rate? _____

Gravity and Acceleration

The acceleration of a freely falling body is 9.8 m/s/s (or 9.8 m/s²) due to the force of gravity.

Using the formula $a = \dfrac{v_f - v_i}{t}$, we can calculate the velocity of a falling object at any time if the initial velocity is known.

Example: What is the velocity of a rubber ball dropped from a building roof after 5 seconds?

$$9.8 \text{ m/s}^2 = \frac{v_f - 0}{5 \text{ s}}$$
$$v_f = 49 \text{ m/s}$$

Solve each problem.

1.	What is the velocity of a quarter dropped from a tower after 10 s?
2.	If a block of wood dropped from a tall building has attained a velocity of 78.4 m/s, how long has it been falling?
3.	If a ball that is freely falling has attained a velocity of 19.6 m/s after 2 s, what is its velocity 5 s later?
4.	A piece of metal has attained a velocity of 107.8 m/s after falling for 10 s. What is its initial velocity?
5.	How long will it take an object that falls from rest to attain a velocity of 147 m/s?

Gravity, Acceleration, and Distance

The distance covered by a freely falling body is calculated by the following formula:

$$d = \frac{at^2}{2}$$

where d = distance
a = acceleration
t = time

Example: How far will an object fall in 5 seconds?

$$d = \frac{(9.8 \text{ m/s}^2)(5 \text{ s})^2}{2} = 122.5 \text{ m}$$

Example: What is the average velocity of a ball that attains a velocity of 39.2 m/s after 4 seconds?

$$v_a = \frac{v_f - v_i}{2} = \frac{39.2 - 0}{2} = 19.6 \text{ m/s}$$

Solve each problem.

1. How far will a rubber ball fall in 10 s? _____

2. How far will a rubber ball fall in 20 s? _____

3. How long will it take an object dropped from a window to fall a distance of 78.4 m? _____

4. What is the final velocity of the ball in problem 1? _____

5. What is the average velocity of the ball in problem 1? _____

6. An airplane is traveling at an altitude of 31,360 m. A box of supplies is dropped from its cargo hold. How long will it take to reach the ground? _____

7. At what velocity will the box in problem 6 be traveling when it hits the ground? _____

8. What is the average velocity of the box in problem 6? _____

Force Diagrams

Find the resultant force in each diagram and draw the resultant vector. Use a ruler and a protractor where necessary. Scale: 1 cm = 10 N, where *N* represents newtons of force.

1. ←— 20 N •——→ 30 N

4.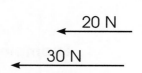

2.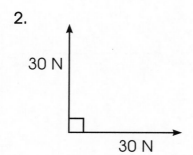

5.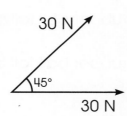

3.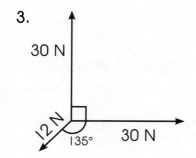

6.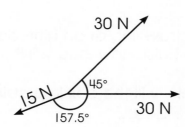

Force and Acceleration

A **force** is a push or a pull. To calculate force, we use the following formula:

$$F = ma$$

where F = force (N)
m = mass (kg)
a = acceleration (m/s^2)

Example: With what force will a rubber ball hit the ground if it has a mass of 0.25 kg?

$$F = (0.25 \text{ kg})(9.8 \text{ m/s}^2)$$
$$F = 2.45 \text{ N}$$

Solve each problem.

1.	With what force will a car hit a tree if the car has a mass of 3,000 kg and it is accelerating at a rate of 2 m/s^2?
2.	A 10-kg bowling ball would require what force to accelerate it down an alleyway at a rate of 3 m/s^2?
3.	What is the mass of a falling rock if it hits the ground with a force of 147 N?
4.	What is the acceleration of a softball if it has a mass of 0.50 kg and hits the catcher's glove with a force of 25 N?
5.	What is the mass of a truck if it is accelerating at a rate of 5 m/s^2 and hits a parked car with a force of 14,000 N?

Motion Matching

Match the term with its definition.

1. _____ kinetic

2. _____ centripetal

3. _____ mass

4. _____ acceleration

5. _____ velocity

6. _____ weight

7. _____ gravity

8. _____ inertia

9. _____ speed

10. _____ momentum

11. _____ newton

A. amount of matter in an object

B. amount of force exerted on an object due to gravity

C. distance covered per unit of time

D. rate at which velocity changes over time

E. speed in a given direction

F. unit of measurement for force

G. energy of motion

H. tendency of a moving object to keep moving

I. depends on the mass and velocity of an object

J. type of force that keeps objects moving in a circle

K. attractive force between two objects

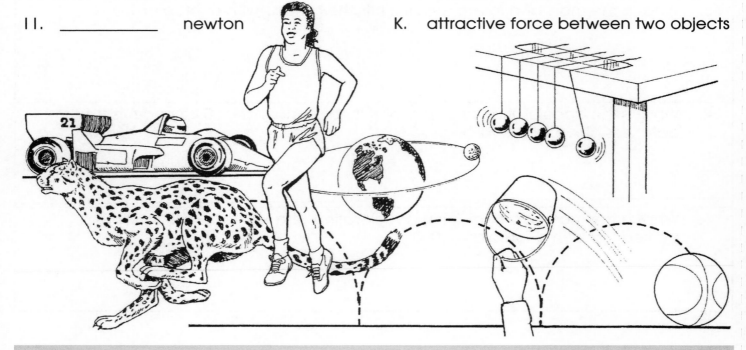

Heat Calculations

Heat is measured in units of joules (J) or calories (cal). The amount of heat given off or absorbed can be calculated by the following formula:

$$\Delta Q = m \times \Delta T \times C$$

heat = (mass in grams)(change in temperature)(specific heat)

The specific heat of water is 1.0 cal/g °C or 4.2 J/g °C.

Solve each problem.

1. How many calories are absorbed by a pot of water with a mass of 500 g in order to raise the temperature from 20°C to 30°C?

2. How many joules would be absorbed for the water in problem 1?

3. If the specific heat of iron is 0.46 J/g C°, how much heat is needed to warm 50 g of iron from 20°C to 100°C?

4. If it takes 105 calories to warm 100 g of aluminum from 20°C to 25°C, what is the specific heat of aluminum?

5. If it takes 31.500 J of heat to warm 750 g of water, what was the temperature change?

Heat and Phase Changes

During a phase change, the temperature remains the same. For these calculations, use the following formulas:

For freezing and melting, heat = (mass in grams)(heat of fusion)

For boiling and condensing, heat = (mass in grams)(heat of vaporization)

The heat of fusion of water is 340 J/g.
The heat of vaporization of water is 2,300 J/g.

Solve each problem.

1.	How many joules of heat are necessary to melt 500 g of ice at its freezing point?
2.	How many kilojoules is this?
3.	How much heat is necessary to vaporize 500 g of water at its boiling point?
4.	If 5,100 J of heat are given off when a sample of water freezes, what is the mass of the water?
5.	If 57,500 J of heat are given off when a sample of steam condenses, what is the mass of the steam?

Simple Machines

Identify the type of simple machine shown in each picture.

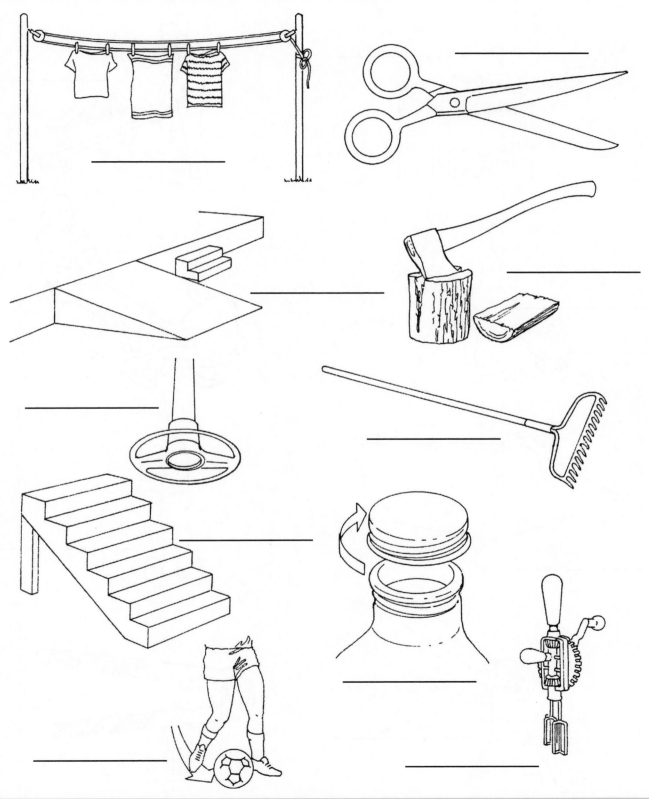

Types of Levers

Classify each lever as *first*, *second*, or *third class*.

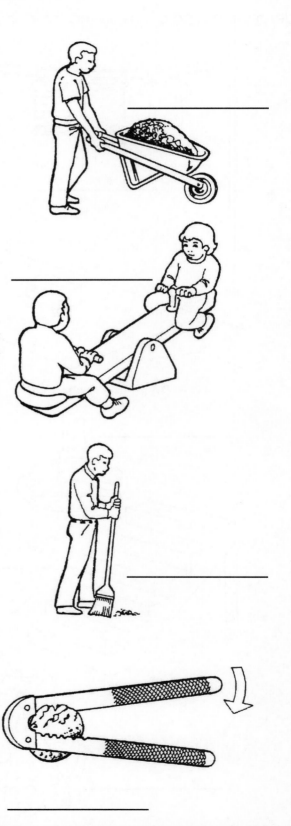

Name_____

Potential and Kinetic Energy

Potential energy is stored energy due to position. **Kinetic energy** is energy that depends on mass and velocity (movement).

For a closed system, the sum of the potential energy and the kinetic energy is a constant. As the potential energy decreases, the kinetic energy increases.

potential energy $=$ weight × height
(P.E. $= w \times h$)

kinetic energy $=$ $\frac{1}{2}$ mass × velocity^2
(K.E. $= \frac{1}{2} mv^2$)

units used:
energy	$=$	joules (J)
weight	$=$	newtons (N)
height	$=$	meters (m)
mass	$=$	kilograms (kg)
velocity	$=$	meters per second (m/s)

Solve each problem.

1.	What is the potential energy of a rock that weighs 100 N that is sitting on top of a hill 300 m high?
2.	What is the kinetic energy of a bicycle with a mass of 14 kg traveling at a velocity of 3 m/s?
3.	A flower pot weighing 3 N is sitting on a windowsill 30 m from the ground. Is the energy of the flower pot potential or kinetic? How much energy does it possess?
4.	When the flower pot in problem 3 is only 10 m from the ground, what is its potential energy?
5.	How much of the total energy in problems 3 and 4 has been transformed to kinetic energy?
6.	A 1,200-kg automobile is traveling at a velocity of 100 m/s. Is its energy potential or kinetic? How much energy does it possess?

Calculating Work

Work has a special meaning in science. It is the product of the force applied to an object and the distance the object moves. The unit of work is the joule (J).

$$\text{work} = \text{force (N)} \times \text{distance (m)}$$
$$W = F \times D$$

Solve each problem.

1.	A book weighing 1.0 N is lifted 2 m. How much work was done?
2.	A force of 15 M is used to push a box along the floor a distance of 3 m. How much work was done?
3.	It took 50 J to push a chair 5 m across the floor. With what force was the chair pushed?
4.	A force of 100 N was necessary to lift a rock. A total of 150 J of work was done. How far was the rock lifted?
5.	It took 500 N of force to push a car 4 m. How much work was done?
6.	A young man exerted a force of 9,000 N on a stalled car but was unable to move it. How much work was done?

Mechanical Advantage

$$MA = \frac{F_R}{F_E}$$

where F_R = resistance force
F_E = effort force

Identify the mechanical advantage of each simple machine.

1.
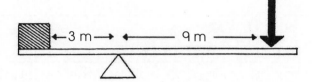

_____

2.
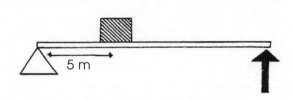

_____

3.
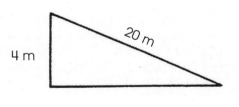

_____

4.
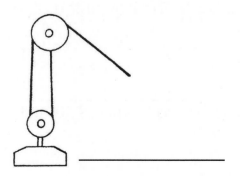 _____

5.
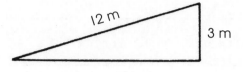

_____

6.
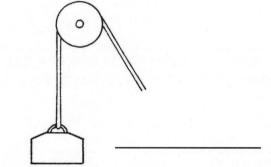 _____

7.
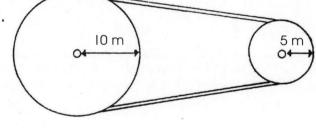

_____

8.
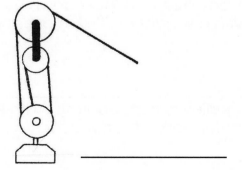 _____

Calculating Efficiency

The amount of work obtained from a machine is always less than the amount of work put into it. This is because some of the work is lost due to friction. The efficiency of a machine can be calculated using the following formula.

$$\text{percent efficiency} = \frac{\text{work output}}{\text{work input}} \times 100$$

Find the efficiency of each machine.

1.	A man expends 100 J of work to move a box up an inclined plane. The amount of work produced is 80 J.
2.	A box weighing 100 N is pushed up an inclined plane that is 5 m long. It takes a force of 75 N to push it to the top, which has a height of 3 m.
3.	Using a lever, a person applies 60 N of force and moves the lever 1 m. This moves a 200-newton rock at the other end by 0.2 m.
4.	A person in a wheelchair exerts a force of 25 N to go up a ramp that is 10 m long. The weight of the person and wheelchair is 60 N and the height of the ramp is 3 m.
5.	A boy pushes a lever down 2 m with a force of 75 N. The box at the other end, with a weight of 50 N, moves up 2.5 m.
6.	A pulley system operates with 40% efficiency. If the work put in is 200 J, how much useful work is produced?

Calculating Power

Power is the amount of work done per unit of time. The unit for power, joules/second, is the watt.

$$\text{power} = \frac{\text{work}}{\text{time}}$$

work = joules (J)

time = seconds (s)

Solve each problem.

1.	A set of pulleys is used to lift a piano weighing 1,000 N. The piano is lifted 3 m in 60 s. How much power is used?
2.	How much power is used if a force of 35 N is used to push a box a distance of 10 m in 5 s?
3.	What is the power of a kitchen blender if it can perform 3,750 J of work in 15 s?
4.	How much work is done using a 500-watt microwave oven for 5 minutes?
5.	How much work is done using a 60-watt lightbulb for 1 hour?

Force and Work Crossword

Across

3. Force times distance
4. Point around which a lever rotates
5. Amount of work done per unit of time
6. Can be considered a type of inclined plane wrapped around a cylinder
7. A machine makes work easier by reducing force and increasing _____ .
9. How many times a force is multiplied by a machine is the mechanical _____ .
11. An inclined plane is an example of a _____ machine.
12. An automobile is an example of this type of machine.

Down

1. Unit of force
2. Unit for work (newton-meter)
4. Force that reduces the efficiency of a machine
8. Joules per second
10. Work output divided by work input

Name_____   35

Wave Diagram

Label the diagram with the following terms: *amplitude, wavelength, crest, trough,* and *rest position*.

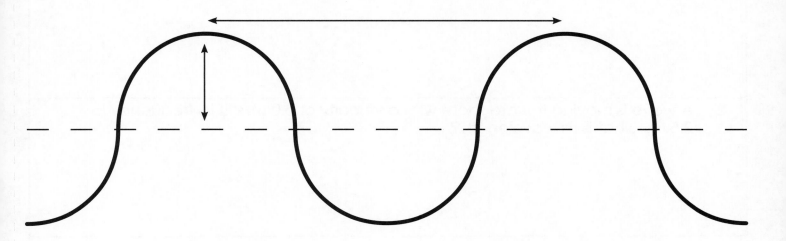

Define each term.

amplitude _____

_____

wavelength _____

_____

crest _____

_____

trough _____

_____

Wave Velocity Calculations

velocity (m/s) = wavelength (m) × frequency (Hz)

Solve each problem.

1. A tuning fork has a frequency of 280 hertz (Hz), and the wavelength of the sound produced is 1.5 m. Calculate the velocity of the wave.

2. A wave is moving toward shore with a velocity of 5.0 m/s. If its frequency is 2.5 Hz, what is its wavelength?

3. The speed of light is about 3.0×10^8 m/s. Red light has a wavelength of about 6.5×10^{-7} m. What is its frequency?

4. The frequency of violet light is 7.5×10^{14} Hz. What is its wavelength?

5. A jump rope is shaken, producing a wave with a wavelength of 0.5 m. The crest of the wave passes a certain point 4 times per second. What is the velocity of the wave?

Sound and Music Crossword

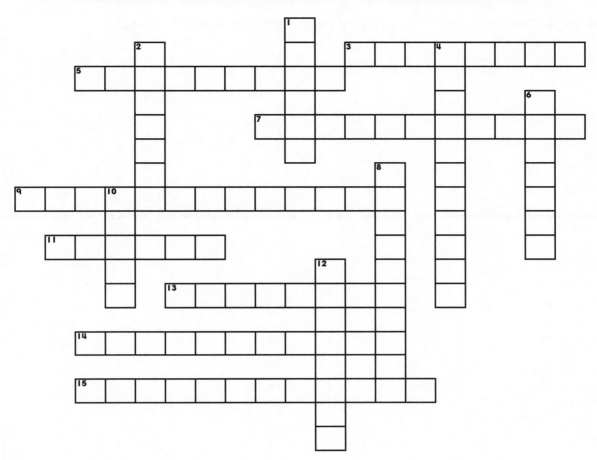

Across

3. Has a higher frequency than the fundamental frequency

5. The control of noise and the vibrations that cause noise

7. The lowest frequency in a musical sound

9. Type of wave in which matter vibrates in the same direction that the wave travels

11. A set of eight notes on the musical scale

13. As the amplitude of sound waves increases, the _____ of the sound increases.

14. Area where sound waves are pushed together

15. The combination of two or more sound waves can cause _____.

Down

1. Sound does not travel through a _____.

2. This effect is a change in wave frequency caused by the motion of the source of the wave.

4. Area where sound waves are pushed apart

6. Produced when overtones have frequencies that are whole number multiples of the fundamental frequency

8. Sounds that cannot be heard by human beings

10. This depends on the frequency of the sound waves.

12. The intensity of sounds are measured in units called _____.

Reflection

Draw the expected path of the light ray as it reflects off each mirror.

1.

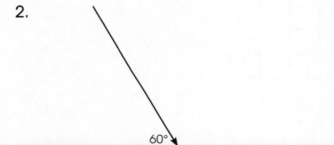

4.

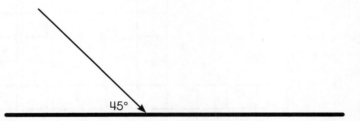

2.

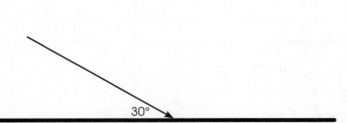

5.

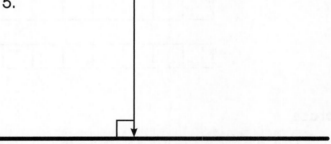

3.

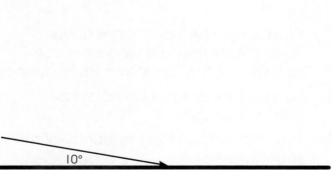

6.

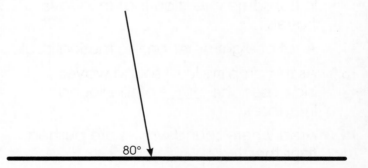

Refraction

Draw the pathway of the light beam as it passes through each substance. Using a protractor, measure the refracted angle.

A.

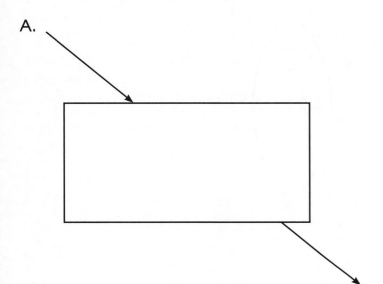

| Which substance has the greatest index of refraction? _____ |

B.

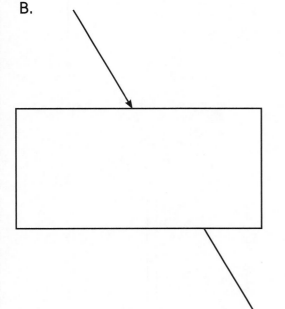

C.

Light Rays and Convex Lenses

Draw the pathway of the light from the object on the left through the convex lense. Label the focal point and the inverted image.

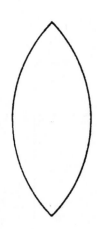

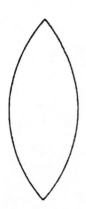

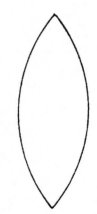

Light Rays and Concave Lenses

Draw the pathway of the light from the object on the left through the concave lens. Label the image and the focal point.

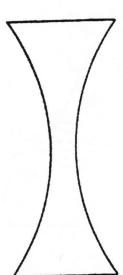

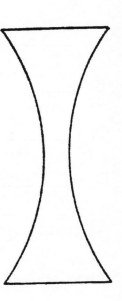

White Light Spectrum

Label the colors coming through the prism as the white light is reflected through it.

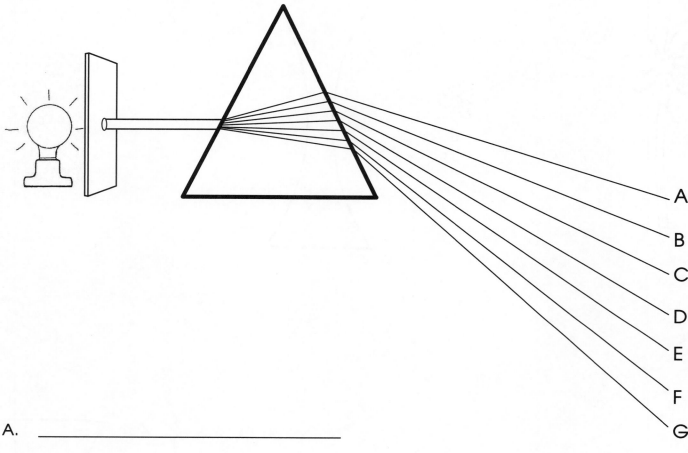

A. _____

B. _____

C. _____

D. _____

E. _____

F. _____

G. _____

Name_____

Light Matching

Match the word with the correct definition or corresponding phrase.

1. _____ hertz

2. _____ wave velocity

3. _____ frequency

4. _____ reflection

5. _____ wavelength

6. _____ refraction

7. _____ crest

8. _____ trough

9. _____ photon

10. _____ light

11. _____ prism

12. _____ index of refraction

13. _____ angle of incidence

14. _____ angle of reflection

15. _____ visible light spectrum

16. _____ normal

A. the angle at which a ray "bounces off" of a surface

B. bending of light waves when they pass through another substance

C. an imaginary line drawn at a right angle to the surface of a barrier

D. number of waves that pass a given point in one second

E. tells how much a ray of light will bend as it travels through a given material

F. translucent material that separates white light into colors

G. frequency times wavelength

H. lowest part of a wave

I. type of electromagnetic radiation

J. unit for frequency

K. the bouncing of a wave off another object

L. a continuous band of colors arranged according to wavelength or frequency

M. distance between corresponding points on two waves

N. a particle of light

O. highest point of a wave

P. the angle at which a ray of light strikes a surface

© Carson-Dellosa • CD-104642

43

Magnetic Fields

Draw the pattern of magnetic fields around each magnet.

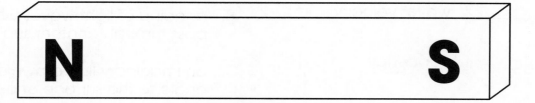

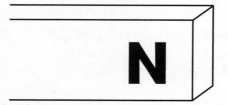 

Calculating Current

Ohm's Law states that $I = \dfrac{V}{R}$

where I = current (amperes, A)
        V = voltage (volts, V)
        R = resistance (ohms, Ω)

Solve each problem.

1. What is the current produced with a 9-volt battery through a resistance of 100 ohms?

2. Find the current when a 12-volt battery is connected through a resistance of 25 ohms.

3. If the potential difference is 120 V and the resistance is 50 ohms, what is the current?

4. What would be the current in problem 3 if the potential difference were doubled?

5. What would be the current in problem 3 if the resistance were doubled?

Calculating Voltage

V	$=$	I	$\times$	R
voltage (volts, V)	=	current (amperes, A)	$\times$	Resistance (ohms, Ω)

Solve each problem.

1. What voltage produces a current of 50 A with a resistance of 20 ohms?

2. Silver has a resistance of 1.98×10^{-4} ohms. What voltage would produce a current of 100 A?

3. A current of 250 A is flowing through a copper wire with a resistance of 2.09×10^{-4} ohms. What is the voltage?

4. What voltage produces a current of 500 A with a resistance of 50 ohms?

5. What voltage would produce a current of 100 A through an aluminum wire that has a resistance of 3.44×10^{-4} ohms?

Calculating Resistance

$$R = \frac{V}{I} \qquad \text{resistance (ohms)} = \frac{\text{voltage (V)}}{\text{current (A)}}$$

Solve each problem.

1. What resistance would produce a current of 200 A with a potential difference of 2,000 V?

2. A 12-volt battery produces a current of 25 A. What is the resistance?

3. A 9-volt battery produces a current of 2.0 A. What is the resistance?

4. An overhead wire has a potential difference of 2,000 V. If the current flowing through the wire is one million amperes, what is the resistance of the wire?

5. What is the resistance of a lightbulb if a 120-volt potential difference produces a current of 0.8 A?

Ohm's Law Problems

Using Ohm's Law, solve each problem.

1. What is the current produced by a potential difference of 240 V through a resistance of 0.2 ohms?

2. What resistance would produce a current of 120 A from a 6-volt battery?

3. What voltage is necessary to produce a current of 200 A through a resistance of 1×10^{-3} ohms?

4. What is the current produced by a 9-volt battery flowing through a resistance of 2×10^{-4} ohms?

5. What is the potential difference if a resistance of 25 ohms produces a current of 250 A?

Calculating Power

P	$=$	V	$\times$	I
power (watts, W)	=	voltage (volts, V)	×	current (amperes, A)

Solve each problem.

1. A 6-volt battery produces a current of 0.5 A. What is the power in the circuit?

2. A 100-watt light bulb is operating on 1.2 A current. What is the voltage?

3. A potential difference of 120 V is operating on a 500-watt microwave oven. What is the current being used?

4. A lightbulb uses 0.625 A from a source of 120 V. How much power is used by the bulb?

5. What voltage is necessary to run a 500-watt motor with a current of 200 A?

Name_____

Calculating Electrical Energy and Cost

Electrical energy is usually measured in units of kilowatt-hours (kWh). One kilowatt-hour is 1,000 watts of power for one hour of time.

Example: A coffee pot operates on 2 amps of current on a 110-volt circuit for 3 hours. Calculate the total kWh used.

1. Determine power. $P = V \times I$
$$= 110\,V \times 2\,A$$
$$= 220\,W$$

$kWh = P \times hours$

$$kWh = \frac{V \times I \times hours}{1,000}$$

2. Convert watts to kilowatts.

$$220\ watts \times \frac{1\ kilowatt}{1,000\ watts} = 0.22\ kW$$

3. Multiply by the hours given in the problem.

$$0.22\ kW \times 3\ hr = 0.66\ kWh$$

Solve each problem.

1. A microwave oven operates on 5 amps of current on a 110-volt circuit for one hour. Calculate the total kilowatt-hours used. _____

2. How much would it cost to run the microwave in problem 1 if the cost of energy is $0.10 per kWh? _____

3. An electric stove operates on 20 amps of current on a 220-volt circuit for one hour. Calculate the total kilowatt-hours used. _____

4. What is the cost of using the stove in problem 3 if the cost of energy if $0.10 per kWh? _____

5. A refrigerator operates on 15 amps of current on a 220-volt circuit for 18 hours per day. How many kilowatt hours are used per day? _____

6. If the electric costs are 15¢ per kWh, how much does it cost to run the refrigerator in problem 5 per day? _____

7. The meter reading on June 1 was 84,502 kWh. On July 1, the meter read 87,498 kWh. If the cost of electricity in the area was 12¢ per kWh, what was the electric bill for the month of June? _____

8. A room was lighted with 3 100-watt bulbs for 5 hours per day. If the cost of electricity was 9¢ per kWh, how much would be saved per day by switching to 60-watt bulbs? _____

Series and Parallel Circuits

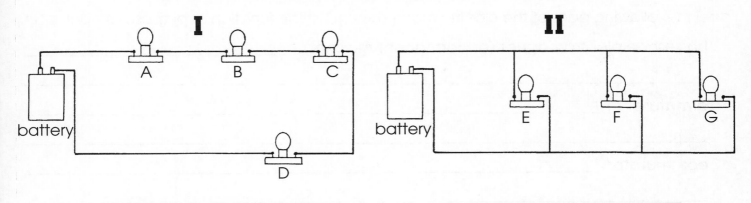

I

A   B   C

battery

D

II

battery

E   F   G

Answer the following questions about circuits I and II above.

1. Label circuits I and II as *series* or *parallel*.

2. If bulb A burns out, will bulb D still light? _____

3. If bulb F burns out, will bulb G still light? _____

4. If bulbs B, C, and D are burned out, will bulb A still light? _____

5. If bulbs F and G are missing, will bulb E still light? _____

6. Draw a diagram of a parallel circuit with 3 lightbulbs, 3 switches, and a battery. Each lightbulb is on a separate switch.

7. Draw a diagram of a series circuit with 3 lightbulbs, one switch, and a battery.

8. Would series or parallel circuits be better for wiring light in a house? _____

    Why? _____

    _____

An Electric Motor

Label the following parts of the electric motor shown. List the function or purpose of each part.

horseshoe electromagnet (or permanent magnet) _____

_____

armature _____

_____

commutator _____

_____

brushes (+ and –) _____

_____

field coil _____

_____

current source _____

_____

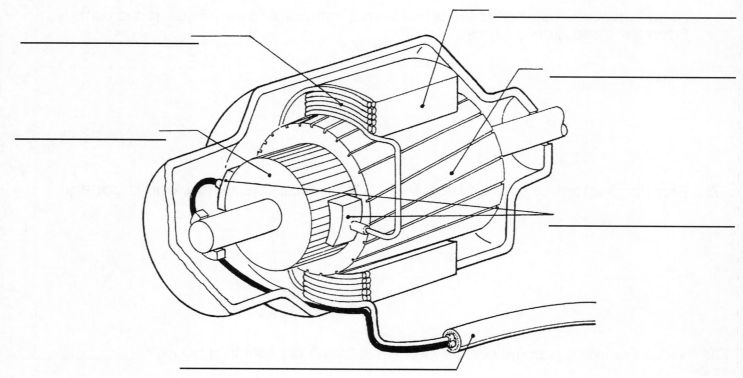

An Electric Generator

Label the parts of an alternating current and a direct current generator. List the function or purpose of each part.

wire coils _____

_____

brushes _____

_____

slip rings (ac only) _____

_____

commutator (dc only) _____

_____

armature _____

_____

magnet _____

_____

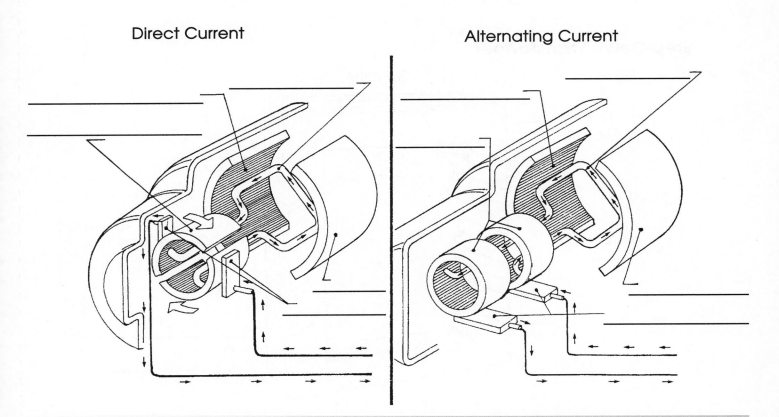

Direct Current   Alternating Current

Transformers

Determine the voltage and current in each transformer.

Step-Up Transformer

1:2 ratio

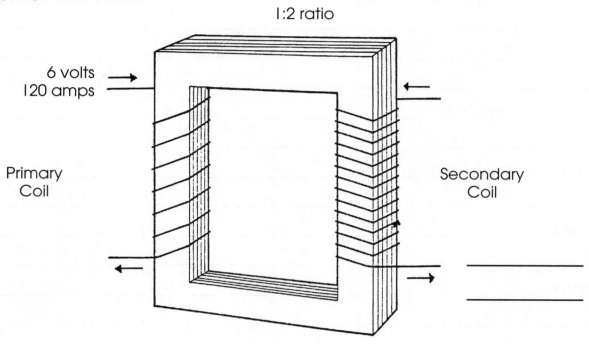

6 volts
120 amps →

Primary
Coil

Secondary
Coil

Step-Down Transformer

3:1 ratio

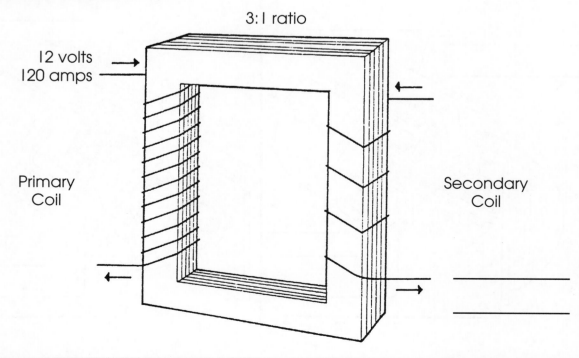

12 volts
120 amps →

Primary
Coil

Secondary
Coil

Electricity Crossword

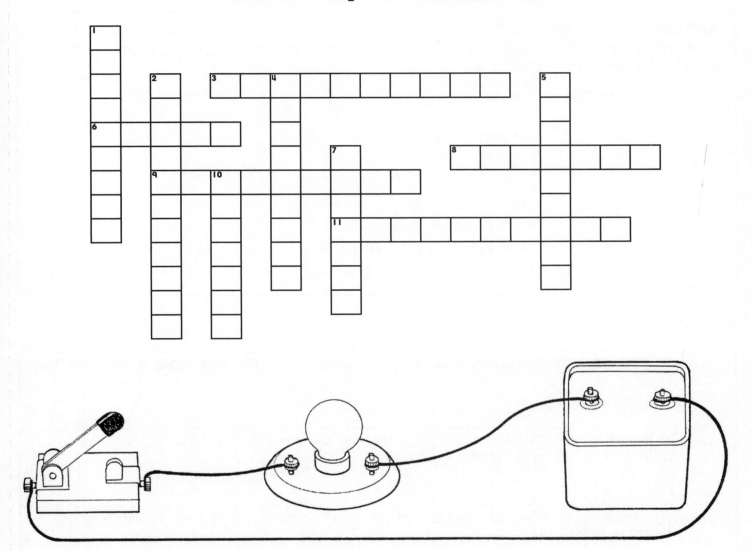

Across

3. Made from semiconductors and needs little voltage
6. An electric _____ converts electrical energy to mechanical energy.
8. Unit for measuring current
9. Changes alternating current to direct
11. This type of circuit may contain billions of tiny transistors.

Down

1. Measures potential difference
2. Current that changes direction
4. Magnifies a small electric signal
5. A device that converts mechanical energy into electricity
7. A semiconductor material
10. A device that uses electrons to produce images on a screen is a _____ ray tube.

Half-Life Calculations

Half-life is the time required for one-half of radioactive nuclei to decay (change to another element). It is possible to calculate the amount of a radioactive element that will be left if we know its half-life.

Example: The half-life of Po-214 is 0.001 second. How much of a 10-g sample will be left after 0.003 seconds?

Calculate the number of half-lives:

$$0.003 \text{ seconds} \times \frac{1 \text{ half-life}}{0.001 \text{ second}} = 3 \text{ half-lives}$$

After 0 half-lives, 10 g are left.

After 1 half-life, 5 g are left.

After 2 half-lives, 2.5 g are left.

After 3 half-lives, 1.25 g are left.

Solve each problem.

1.	The half-life of radon-222 is 3.8 days. How much of a 100-g sample is left after 15.2 days?
2.	Carbon-14 has a half-life of 5,730 years. If a sample contains 70 mg originally, how much is left after 17,190 years?
3.	How much of a 500-g sample of potassium-42 is left after 62 hours? The half-life of K-42 is 12.4 hours.
4.	The half-life of cobalt-60 is 5.26 years. If 50 g are left after 15.8 years, how many grams were in the original sample?
5.	The half-life of I-131 is 8.07 days. If 25 g are left after 40.35 days, how many grams were in the original sample?
6.	If 100 g of Au-198 decays to 6.25 g in 10.8 days, what is the half-life of Au-198?

A Nuclear Reactor

Label the parts of a nuclear reactor. List the function or purpose of each part.

control rods _____

_____

_____

reaction chamber _____

_____

_____

moderator _____

_____

_____

coolant _____

_____

_____

shield _____

_____

_____

turbine generator _____

_____

_____

fuel _____

_____

_____

transformer _____

_____

_____

heat exchanger _____

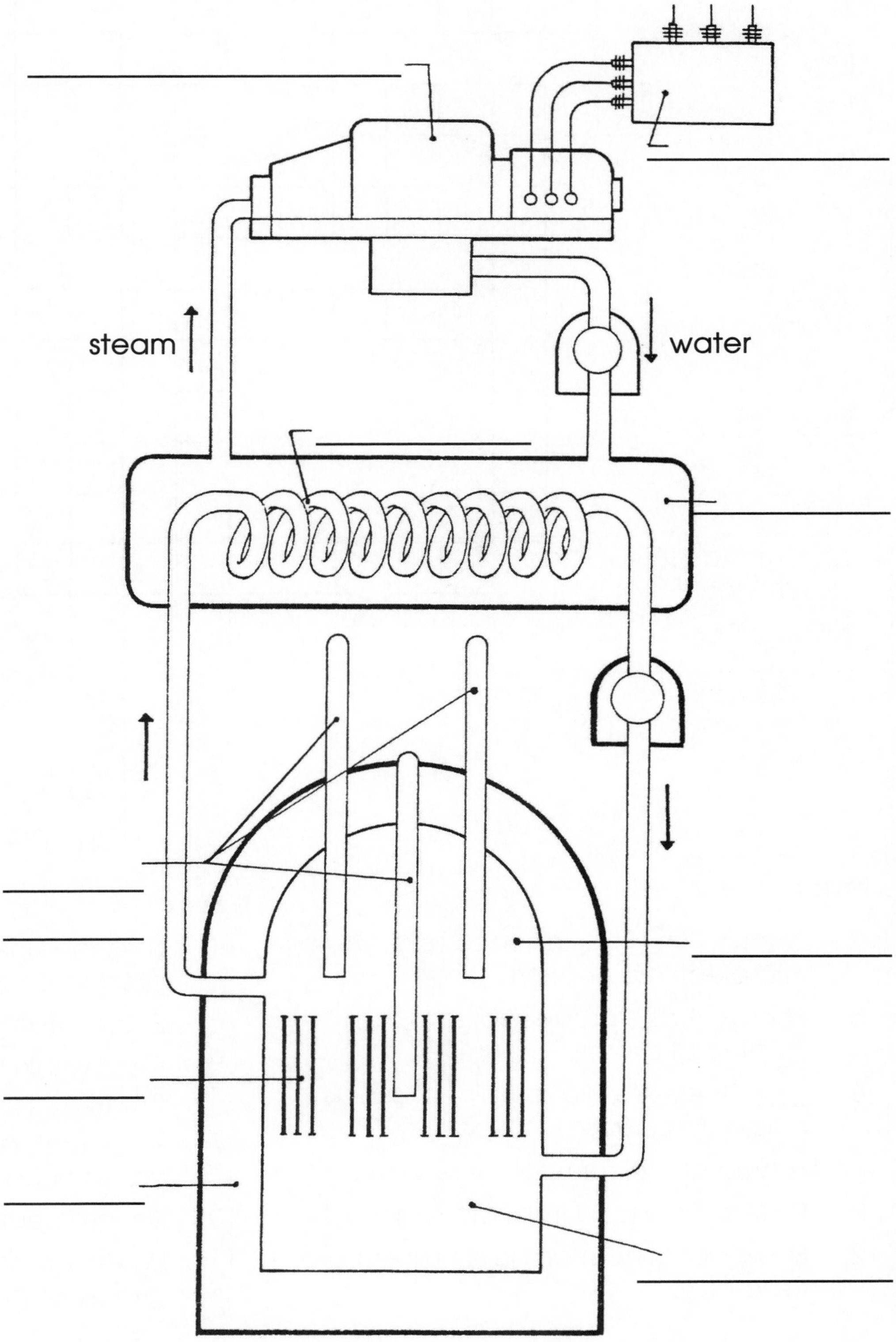

_____

steam ↑

↓ water

Fuel Alternatives Crossword

Across

2. Solar _____ change light energy into electrical energy.

5. Energy that is produced from the splitting of atoms

6. _____ fuels are the remains of plants and animals from long ago.

8. A type of fuel for nuclear reactors

9. Power produced from moving water

12. Slows down neutrons in a nuclear reactor

Down

1. Uses the kinetic energy of moving air to produce power

3. Energy from the sun

4. Heat within Earth is called _____ energy.

7. _____ fuels are made from materials like plants or coal.

10. Absorb neutrons in a nuclear reactor

11. Power produced from the pull of gravity of the moon and sun

Substances and Mixtures

A **substance** is matter for which a chemical formula can be written. Elements and compounds are substances. **Mixtures** can be in any proportion, and the parts are not chemically bonded.

Classify each item as a mixture or substance by writing *M* or *S* in the space provided.

1.	sodium	_____	11.	iron	_____
2.	water	_____	12.	salt water	_____
3.	soil	_____	13.	ice cream	_____
4.	coffee	_____	14.	nitrogen	_____
5.	oxygen	_____	15.	eggs	_____
6.	alcohol	_____	16.	blood	_____
7.	carbon dioxide	_____	17.	table salt	_____
8.	cake batter	_____	18.	nail polish	_____
9.	air	_____	19.	milk	_____
10.	soup	_____	20.	cola	_____

Homogeneous vs. Heterogeneous Matter

Classify each substance or mixture as either homogeneous or heterogeneous. Place a check in the correct column.

	Homogeneous	Heterogeneous
1. flat soda pop		
2. cherry vanilla ice cream		
3. salad dressing		
4. sugar		
5. soil		
6. aluminum foil		
7. black coffee		
8. sugar water		
9. city air		
10. paint		
11. alcohol		
12. iron		
13. beach sand		
14. pure air		
15. spaghetti sauce		

Solutions, Colloids, and Suspensions

Label each mixture as a *solution*, *colloid*, or *suspension*. Then, give an example of each.

1. large particles,
    settles out on standing

Kind of mixture: _____

Example: _____

_____

2. medium-sized particles,
    does not settle out on
    standing, scatters light

Kind of mixture: _____

Example: _____

_____

3. very small particles,
    does not settle out on standing

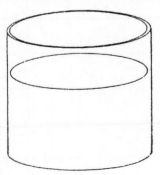

Kind of mixture: _____

Example: _____

_____

Physical vs. Chemical Properties

A **physical property** is observed with the senses and can be determined without changing the indentity of the object. For example, color, shape, mass, length, density, specific heat, and odor are all examples of physical properties.

A **chemical property** indicates how a substance reacts with something else. The original substance is fundamentally changed in observing a chemical property. For example, the ability of iron to rust is a chemical property. The iron has reacted with oxygen, and the original iron metal is changed. It now exists as iron oxide, a different substance.

Classify each property as either chemical or physical by placing a check mark in the appropriate column.

		Physical Property	Chemical Property
1.	red color		
2.	density		
3.	flammability		
4.	solubility		
5.	reacts with acid to form hydrogen		
6.	supports combustion		
7.	bitter taste		
8.	melting point		
9.	reacts with water to form a gas		
10.	reacts with a base to form water		
11.	hardness		
12.	boiling point		
13.	can neutralize a base		
14.	luster		
15.	odor		

Physical vs. Chemical Changes

In a **physical change**, the original substance still exists; it only changes in form. In a **chemical change**, a new substance is produced. Energy changes always accompany chemical changes.

Classify each as a *physical* or *chemical* change.

1. Sodium hydroxide dissolves in water. _____

2. Hydrochloric acid reacts with potassium hydroxide to produce a salt, water, and heat. _____

3. A pellet of sodium is sliced in two. _____

4. Water is heated and changed to steam. _____

5. Potassium chlorate decomposes to potassium chloride and oxygen gas.
_____

6. Iron rusts. _____

7. Ice melts. _____

8. Acid on limestone produces carbon dioxide gas. _____

9. Milk sours. _____

10. Wood rots. _____

Separation of Mixtures

Taking advantage of various physical and chemical properties, describe how you would separate the following mixtures into their components.

1. sand and water _____

_____

_____

2. sugar and water _____

_____

_____

3. oil and water _____

_____

_____

4. sand and gravel _____

_____

_____

5. a mixture of heptane (boiling point 98°C) and heptanol (boiling point 176°C)

_____

_____

6. a mixture of iodine solid and sodium chloride (Hint: Iodine is not soluble in water.)

_____

_____

7. a mixture of lead and aluminum pellets _____

_____

_____

8. a mixture of salt and iron filings _____

_____

_____

Name_____

States of Matter Crossword

Across

3. Change of a gas to a liquid
6. This type of property can be observed without destroying the substance.
7. Mass of a substance divided by unit volume
8. Physical change of a solid to a liquid at the melting point
9. State of matter having no definite volume or shape
10. Homogeneous mixture
12. This type of change produces a new substance.
13. Change of a liquid to a solid

Down

1. Anything that has mass and takes up space
2. State in which atoms or molecules are very close together and are regularly arranged
4. Change of a liquid to a gas
5. This state of matter consists of electrically charged particles.
10. Elements and compounds
11. State of matter having a definite volume but no definite shape

Elements and Their Symbols

Identify the symbol for each element.

1. oxygen _____
2. hydrogen _____
3. chlorine _____
4. sodium _____
5. fluorine _____
6. carbon _____
7. helium _____
8. nitrogen _____
9. copper _____
10. sulfur _____

11. magnesium _____
12. manganese _____
13. neon _____
14. bromine _____
15. phosphorus _____
16. silver _____
17. lead _____
18. iron _____
19. calcium _____
20. potassium _____

Identify the name of the element that corresponds to each symbol.

21. Cu _____
22. K _____
23. C _____
24. Au _____
25. Zn _____
26. Pb _____
27. Fe _____
28. Na _____
29. S _____
30. Al _____

31. Ca _____
32. Ag _____
33. P _____
34. O _____
35. I _____
36. Sn _____
37. H _____
38. F _____
39. Ni _____
40. Hg _____

Elements and Minerals Crossword

Across

2. Element on which life is based
4. Its low melting point is useful in emergency fire sprinkler systems.
6. Its common allotropes are red and white.
11. This nonmental in Group 16 is a good conductor.
12. Halogen found in seawater
13. Most abundant halogen
14. Gas used in lighted signs to produce a red color

Down

1. Most abundant element in air
3. Fire-resistant material no longer used due to its carcinogenicity
5. Light element used for lifting airships
7. Ozone is an allotrope of this element.
8. Element responsible for the odor of rotten eggs
9. Poisonous element that is also used in medicines and rat poison
10. Most reactive nonmetal

Parts of an Atom

An atom is made up of protons and neutrons, which are in the nucleus, and electrons, which are in the electron cloud surrounding the atom.

The **atomic number** equals the number of protons. The electrons in a neutral atom equal the number of protons. The mass number equals the sum of the protons and neutrons.

The **charge** indicates the number of electrons that have been lost or gained. A positive charge indicates the number of electrons (which are negatively charged) lost. A negative charge indicates the number of electrons gained. This structure can be written as part of a chemical symbol.

mass number → $^{12}_{6}C^{+4}$ ← charge

atomic number →

This carbon ion would have 6 protons, 6 neutrons, and 2 electrons.

Complete the chart.

Element/ Ion	Atomic Number	Mass Number	Charge	Protons	Neutrons	Electrons
$^{24}_{12}Mg$						
$^{39}_{19}K$						
$^{23}_{11}Na^+$						
$^{19}_{9}F^-$						
$^{27}_{13}Al^{3+}$						
$^{1}_{1}H$						
$^{24}Mg^{2+}$						
Ag						
S^{2-}						
$^{2}_{1}H$						
$^{35}Cl^-$						
Be^{2+}						

Bohr Models

Draw a Bohr model for each atom.

I. ^1_1H	4. ^4_2He
2. ^7_3Li	5. $^{23}_{11}\text{Na}$
3. $^{35}_{17}\text{Cl}$	6. $^{64}_{29}\text{Cu}$

Properties of Metals and Nonmetals

For each physical or chemical property, put a check in the appropriate column if it applies to a metal or a nonmetal.

Property	Metal	Nonmetal
1. malleable		
2. lustrous		
3. gaseous at room temperature		
4. forms negative ions		
5. metallic bonding		
6. more than 4 valence electrons		
7. conducts electricity in a solid state		
8. ductile		
9. brittle		
10. only forms positive ions		
11. nonconductor		
12. covalent bonding		
13. can have both positive and negative oxidation numbers		
14. gives away electrons in chemical reactions		
15. prefers to receive electrons in chemical reactions		

Activity of the Elements

Since metals prefer to give away electrons during chemical bonding, the most active metals are closest to francium, which is a large atom with low ionization energy and electronegativity. Nonmetals prefer to pull in electrons, so the most active nonmetals are closest to fluorine, which has a high ionization energy and electronegativity. The noble gases (Group 18) are considered inactive since they already have a stable octet of electrons in their outer shell.

Referring to a periodic table, circle the member of each pair of elements which is most chemically active.

1.	Li	and	Na	16.	Cl_2 and Br_2	
2.	Cl_2	and	F_2	17.	Xe and I_2	
3.	N_2	and	N	18.	Fe and Ra	
4.	Rb	and	Ca	19.	Sr and Mn	
5.	Ti	and	Ca	20.	K and Na	
6.	K	and	Mg	21.	Au and Mg	
7.	O_2	and	S	22.	S and Rn	
8.	I_2	and	Br_2	23.	Li and Be	
9.	Na	and	Zn	24.	Se and Br_2	
10.	P	and	S	25.	I_2 and F_2	
11.	N_2	and	O_2	26.	Rb and Sr	
12.	Cl_2	and	Ar	27.	Ba and Ra	
13.	Ba	and	Fr	28.	Na and Mg	
14.	Rb	and	Cu	29.	Te and I_2	
15.	Be	and	Cr	30.	Ca and Rn	

Periodic Table Puzzle

Name_____

| | 1 | 2 | 3 | 4 | 5 | 6 | 7 | 8 | 9 | 10 | 11 | 12 | 13 | 14 | 15 | 16 | 17 | 18 |

Periodic table grid with letters: I (group 1), F (group 2), C (group 1), E (group 9), J (group 13), B (group 14), G (group 16), H (group 17), A (group 18), D (in the inner transition series row).

Place the letter of each of the above elements next to its description.

1. An alkali metal _____

2. An alkaline earth metal _____

3. An inactive gas _____

4. An active nonmetal _____

5. A semimetal _____

6. An inner transition element _____

7. Its most common oxidation state is -2. _____

8. A metal with more than one oxidation state _____

9. A metal with an oxidation number of +3 _____

10. Has oxidation numbers of +1 and -1 _____

Periodic Table Crossword

Across

2. Group I metals
4. Elements in the middle of the periodic table are the _____ metals.
5. The sum of the protons and neutrons is the _____ number.
6. Inactive gases
7. The horizontal rows are called _____.
8. Most of the elements are _____.
10. Nonmetals tend to form _____ ions.

Down

1. Most active nonmetals
2. Group II metals
3. The atomic number is the number of _____.
7. Metals tend to form _____ ions.
9. The elements are arranged by atomic _____.
11. The vertical columns are called families, or _____.

Types of Chemical Bonds

Classify the following compounds as *ionic* (metal and nonmetal), *covalent* (nonmetal and nonmetal), or *both* (compound containing a polyatomic ion).

1. $CaCl_2$ _____

2. CO_2 _____

3. H_2O _____

4. $BaSO_4$ _____

5. K_2O _____

6. NaF _____

7. Na_2CO_3 _____

8. CH_4 _____

9. SO_3 _____

10. $LiBr$ _____

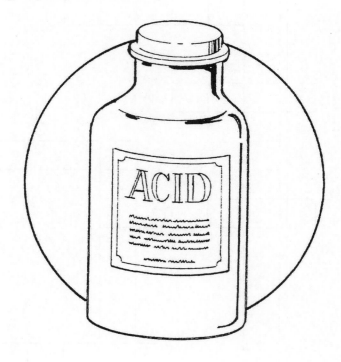

11. MgO _____

12. NH_4Cl _____

13. HCl _____

14. KI _____

15. $NaOH$ _____

16. NO_2 _____

17. $AlPO_4$ _____

18. $FeCl_3$ _____

19. P_2O_5 _____

20. N_2O_3 _____

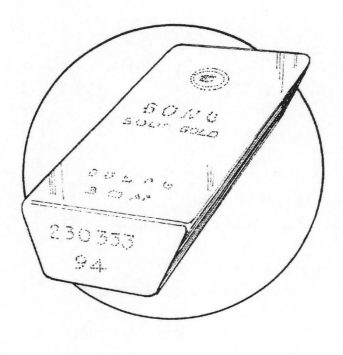

Number of Atoms in a Formula

Determine the number of atoms in each chemical formula.

1. NaCl   _____

2. H_2SO_4 _____

3. KNO_3 _____

4. $CaCl_2$ _____

5. C_2H_6 _____

6. $Ba(OH)_2$ _____

7. NH_4Br _____

8. $Ca_3(PO_4)_2$ _____

9. $Al_2(SO_4)_3$ _____

10. $Mg(NO_3)_2$ _____

11. $Cu(NO_3)_2$ _____

12. $KMnO_4$ _____

13. H_2O_2 _____

14. H_3PO_4 _____

15. $(NH_4)_3PO_4$ _____

16. Fe_2O_3 _____

17. $NaC_2H_3O_2$ _____

18. $Mg(C_2H_3O_2)_2$ _____

19. Hg_2Cl_2 _____

20. K_2SO_3 _____

Gram Formula Mass

Determine the gram formula mass of each compound. Round to the nearest whole number.

1. NaCl   _____

2. H_2SO_4 _____

3. KNO_3 _____

4. $CaCl_2$ _____

5. C_2H_6 _____

6. $Ba(OH)_2$ _____

7. NH_4Br _____

8. $Ca_3(PO_4)_2$ _____

9. $Al_2(SO_4)_3$ _____

10. $Mg(NO_3)_2$ _____

11. $Cu(NO_3)_2$ _____

12. $KMnO_4$ _____

13. H_2O_2 _____

14. H_3PO_4 _____

15. $(NH_4)_3PO_4$ _____

16. Fe_2O_3 _____

17. $NaC_2H_3O_2$ _____

18. $Mg(C_2H_3O_2)_2$ _____

19. Hg_2Cl_2 _____

20. K_2SO_3 _____

Percentage Composition

Solve each problem. Round to the nearest whole number.

1.	What is the percentage of carbon in CO_2?
2.	How many grams of carbon are in 25 g of CO_2?
3.	What is the percentage of sodium in NaCl?
4.	How many grams of sodium are in 75 g of NaCl?
5.	What is the percentage of oxygen in $KClO_3$?
6.	How many grams of oxygen can be obtained from 5.00 g of $KClO_3$?
7.	What is the percentage of silver in $AgNO_3$?
8.	How many grams of silver can be recovered from 125 g of $AgNO_3$?
9.	What is the percentage of gold in $AuCl_3$?
10.	How many grams of gold can be recovered from 35.0 g of $AuCl_3$?

Writing Binary Formulas

Write the formula for the compounds formed from each ion.

1. Na^+, Cl^- _____

2. Ba^{+2}, F^- _____

3. K^+, S^{-2} _____

4. Li^+, Br^- _____

5. Al^{+3}, I^- _____

6. Zn^{+2}, S^{-2} _____

7. Ag^+, O^{-2} _____

8. Mg^{+2}, P^{-3} _____

9. Ni^{+2}, O^{-2} _____

10. Ni^{+3}, O^{-2} _____

11. Fe^{+2}, O^{-2} _____

12. Fe^{+3}, O^{-2} _____

13. Cr^{+2}, S^{-2} _____

14. Cr^{+3}, S^{-2} _____

15. Cu^+, Cl^- _____

16. Cu^{+2}, Cl^- _____

17. Pb^{+2}, O^{-2} _____

18. Pb^{+4}, O^{-2} _____

19. Mn^{+2}, Br^- _____

20. Mn^{+4}, Br^- _____

Naming Binary Compounds (Ionic)

Name each ionic compound, using Roman numerals where necessary.

1. $BaCl_2$ _____

2. NaF _____

3. Ag_2O _____

4. CuBr _____

5. $CuBr_2$ _____

6. FeO _____

7. Fe_2O_3 _____

8. MgS _____

9. Al_2O_3 _____

10. CaI_2 _____

11. K_2S _____

12. $CrCl_2$ _____

13. $CrCl_3$ _____

14. CaO _____

15. Ba_3P_2 _____

16. Hg_2I_2 _____

17. Na_2O _____

18. BeS _____

19. MnO _____

20. Mn_2O_3 _____

Name________________________________

Naming Binary Compounds (Covalent)

Name each compound using the prefix method.

1. CO ________________________________
2. CO_2 ________________________________
3. SO_2 ________________________________
4. NO_2 ________________________________
5. N_2O ________________________________
6. SO_3 ________________________________
7. CCl_4 ________________________________
8. NO ________________________________
9. N_2O_5 ________________________________
10. P_2O_5 ________________________________
11. N_2O_4 ________________________________
12. CS_2 ________________________________
13. OF_2 ________________________________
14. PCl_3 ________________________________
15. PBr_5 ________________________________

Formulas (with Polyatomic Ions)

Matching the horizontal and vertical axes, write the formulas of the compounds with the following combination of ions. The first row is done for you.

	OH^-	NO_3^-	CO_3^{2-}	SO_4^{2-}	PO_4^{3-}
H^+	HOH (H_2O)	HNO_3	H_2CO_3	H_2SO_4	H_3PO_4
Na^+					
Mg^{2+}					
NH_4^+					
Ca^{2+}					
K^+					
Al^{3+}					
Pb^{4+}					

Naming of Non-Binary Compounds

An ionic compound that contains more than two elements must contain a polyatomic ion.

Name each compound.

1. $NaNO_3$ _____

2. $Ca(OH)_2$ _____

3. K_2CO_3 _____

4. NH_4Cl _____

5. $MgSO_4$ _____

6. $AlPO_4$ _____

7. $(NH_4)_2SO_4$ _____

8. Na_3PO_4 _____

9. $CuSO_4$ _____

10. NH_4OH _____

11. Li_2SO_3 _____

12. $Mg(NO_3)_2$ _____

13. $Al(OH)_3$ _____

14. $(NH_4)_3PO_4$ _____

15. KOH _____

16. $Ca(NO_3)_2$ _____

17. K_2SO_4 _____

18. $Pb(OH)_2$ _____

19. Na_2O_2 _____

20. $CuCO_3$ _____

Name________________________________

Naming Compounds (Mixed)

Name each compound.

1. NaCl ________________________________
2. MnS ________________________________
3. K_2O ________________________________
4. $CuBr_2$ ________________________________
5. CuBr ________________________________
6. CO_2 ________________________________
7. $PbSO_4$ ________________________________
8. Li_2CO_3 ________________________________
9. Na_2CO_3 ________________________________
10. NO_2 ________________________________
11. N_2O_4 ________________________________
12. $Ca(OH)_2$ ________________________________
13. NH_4Cl ________________________________
14. SO_3 ________________________________
15. $AlPO_4$ ________________________________
16. CCl_4 ________________________________
17. CaS ________________________________
18. NH_3 ________________________________
19. MgI_2 ________________________________
20. K_3PO_4 ________________________________

Writing Formulas from Names

Write the formula for each compound.

1. carbon monoxide _____

2. sodium chloride _____

3. carbon tetrachloride _____

4. magnesium bromide _____

5. aluminum iodide _____

6. hydrogen hydroxide _____

7. iron(II) fluoride _____

8. carbon dioxide _____

9. sodium carbonate _____

10. ammonium sulfide _____

11. iron(II) oxide _____

12. iron(III) oxide _____

13. magnesium sulfate _____

14. sodium phosphate _____

15. dinitrogen pentoxide _____

16. phosphorus trichloride _____

17. aluminum sulfite _____

18. copper(I) carbonate _____

19. potassium hydrogen carbonate _____

20. sulfur trioxide _____

Balancing Equations

Balance each chemical equation.

1. CH_4 + O_2 $\longrightarrow$ CO_2 + H_2O

2. Na + I_2 $\longrightarrow$ NaI

3. N_2 + O_2 $\longrightarrow$ N_2O

4. N_2 + H_2 $\longrightarrow$ NH_3

5. KI + Cl_2 $\longrightarrow$ KCl + I_2

6. HCl + $Ca(OH)_2$ $\longrightarrow$ $CaCl_2$ + H_2O

7. $KClO_3$ $\longrightarrow$ KCl + O_2

8. K_3PO_4 + HCl $\longrightarrow$ KCl + H_3PO_4

9. S + O_2 $\longrightarrow$ SO_3

10. KI + $Pb(NO_3)_2$ $\longrightarrow$ KNO_3 + PbI_2

11. $CaSO_4$ + $AlBr_3$ $\longrightarrow$ $CaBr_2$ + $Al_2(SO_4)_3$

12. H_2O_2 $\longrightarrow$ H_2O + O_2

13. Na + H_2O $\longrightarrow$ $NaOH$ + H_2

14. C_2H_6 + O_2 $\longrightarrow$ CO_2 + H_2O

15. $Mg(NO_3)_2$ + K_3PO_4 $\longrightarrow$ $Mg_3(PO_4)_2$ + KNO_3

Word Equations

Write and balance each chemical equation.

1. Hydrogen plus oxygen yield water.

2. Nitrogen plus hydrogen yield ammonia.

3. Aluminum bromide plus chlorine yield aluminum chloride and bromine.

4. Hydrochloric acid plus sodium hydroxide yield sodium chloride plus water.

5. Iron plus lead(II) sulfate react forming iron(II) sulfate plus lead.

6. Potassium chlorate, when heated, produces potassium chloride plus oxygen gas.

7. Sulfuric acid decomposes to form sulfur trioxide gas plus water.

8. Sodium oxide combines with water to make sodium hydroxide.

9. Potassium iodide reacts with bromine, forming potassium bromide plus iodine.

10. Sodium phosphate reacts with calcium nitrate to produce sodium nitrate plus calcium phosphate.

11. Zinc reacts with iron(III) chloride yielding zinc chloride plus iron precipitate.

12. Ammonium carbonate and magnesium sulfate react to yield ammonium sulfate plus magnesium carbonate.

13. Phosphoric acid plus calcium hydroxide react, forming solid calcium phosphate plus water.

14. Aluminum plus oxygen gas form aluminum oxide under certain conditions.

15. Nitrogen gas plus oxygen gas react and form dinitrogen pentoxide.

Name_____

Identifying Chemical Reactions

Identify each reaction as *synthesis, decomposition, single replacement,* or *double replacement*.

1. $2KClO_3 \longrightarrow 2KCl + 3O_2$

2. $HCl + NaOH \longrightarrow NaCl + H_2O$

3. $Mg + 2HCl \longrightarrow MgCl_2 + H_2$

4. $2H_2 + O_2 \longrightarrow 2H_2O$

5. $2Al + 3NiBr_2 \longrightarrow 2AlBr_3 + 3Ni$

6. $4Al + 3O_2 \longrightarrow 2Al_2O_3$

7. $2NaCl \longrightarrow 2Na + Cl_2$

8. $CaCl_2 + F_2 \longrightarrow CaF_2 + Cl_2$

9. $AgNO_3 + KCl \longrightarrow AgCl + KNO_3$

10. $N_2 + 3H_2 \longrightarrow 2NH_3$

11. $2H_2O_2 \longrightarrow 2H_2O + O_2$

12. $(NH_4)_2SO_4 + Ba(NO_3)_2 \longrightarrow BaSO_4 + 2NH_4NO_3$

13. $MgI_2 + Br_2 \longrightarrow MgBr_2 + I_2$

14. $SO_3 + H_2O \longrightarrow H_2SO_4$

15. $6KCl + Zn_3(PO_4)_2 \longrightarrow 3ZnCl_2 + 2K_3PO_4$

Name_____

Conservation of Mass

In chemical reactions, mass is neither gained nor lost. The total mass of all the reactants equals the total mass of all the products. Atoms are just rearranged into different compounds.

Using the idea of conservation of mass, solve each problem.

1. $2KClO_3 \longrightarrow 2KCl + 3O_2$

   If 500 g of $KClO_3$ decompresses and produces 303 g of KCl, how many grams of O_2 are produced?

2. $N_2 + 3H_2 \longrightarrow 2NH_3$

   How many grams of H_2 are needed to react with 100 g of N_2 to produce 121 g of NH_3?

3. $4Fe + 3O_2 \longrightarrow 2Fe_2O_3$

   How many grams of oxygen are needed to react with 350 g of iron to produce 500 g of Fe_2O_3?

4. $CH_4 + 2O_2 \longrightarrow CO_2 + 2H_2O$

   Sixteen g of CH_4 react with 64 g of O_2, producing 44 g of CO_2. How many grams of water are produced?

5. $CaCO_3 \longrightarrow CaO + CO_2$

   How much CO_2 is produced from the decomposition of 200 g of $CaCO_3$ if 112 g of CaO are produced?

Mass Relationships in Equations

A balanced equation can tell us the mass relationships involved in a chemical reaction.

Example: $2KClO_3 \qquad 2KCl + 3O_2$

How many grams of KCl are produced if 244 g of $KClO_3$ decompose?

1 formula mass of $KClO_3$ = 122 g

1 formula mass of KCl = 74 g

$$244 \text{ g of } KClO_3 \times \frac{2(74 \text{ g}) \text{ KCl}}{2(122 \text{ g}) KClO_3} = 148 \text{ g KCl}$$

coeffecients from equation

Example: $N_2 + 3H_2 \qquad 2NH_3$

How many grams of H_2 are needed to react with 56 g of N_2?

1 formula mass of N_2 = 28 g

1 formula mass of H_2 = 2 g

$$56 \text{ g } N_2 \times \frac{3(2 \text{ g}) H_2}{1(28 \text{ g}) N_2} = 12 \text{ g}$$

Solve each problem.

1. $2H_2O_2 \longrightarrow 2H_2O + O_2$

   How many grams of water are produced from the decomposition of 68 g of H_2O_2?

   _____

2. How many grams of oxygen are produced in the above reaction?

   _____

3. $2C_2H_6 + 7O_2 \longrightarrow 4CO_2 + 6H_2O$

   How many grams of oxygen are required to completely react with 120 g of C_2H_6?

   _____

4. How many grams of CO_2 are produced in the above reaction?

   _____

5. $2K_3PO_4 + 3MgCl_2 \longrightarrow Mg_3(PO_4)_2 + 6KCl$

   How much $MgCl_2$ is required to react exactly with 500 g of K_3PO_4?

   _____

6. How much KCl will be produced in the above reaction?

   _____

Acid, Base, or Salt?

Identify each compound as an *acid*, a *base*, or a *salt*. Then, indicate whether each acid and base is *strong* or *weak*.

1. HNO_3 _____ _____

2. $NaOH$ _____ _____

3. $NaNO_3$ _____ _____

4. HCl _____ _____

5. KCl _____ _____

6. $Ba(OH)_2$ _____ _____

7. KOH _____ _____

8. H_2S _____ _____

9. $Al(NO_3)_3$ _____ _____

10. H_2SO_4 _____ _____

11. $CaCl_2$ _____ _____

12. H_3PO_4 _____ _____

13. Na_2SO_4 _____ _____

14. $Mg(OH)_2$ _____ _____

15. H_2CO_3 _____ _____

16. NH_4OH _____ _____

17. NH_4Cl _____ _____

18. HBr _____ _____

19. $FeBr_3$ _____ _____

20. HF _____ _____

pH

pH is a measure of the concentration of hydronium ions in a solution. It uses a scale ranging from 0 to 14, with 0 being the most acidic and 14 being the most basic.

Indicators are substances that change color at different pH levels. Phenolphthalein is colorless in an acid and a neutral solution, but pink in a base. Blue litmus changes to red in an acid, and remains blue in neutral and basic solutions. Red litmus remains red in acidic and neutral substances, but turns blue in bases.

Complete the chart.

pH	Acid , Base, or Neutral	Phenolphthalein	Blue Litmus	Red Litmus
2				
8				
4				
7				
13				
11				
5				
1				

Name_____

pH of Salt Solutions

A **salt** is formed from the reaction of an acid and a base.

A strong acid + a strong base $\longrightarrow$ neutral salt

A strong acid + a weak base $\longrightarrow$ acidic salt

A weak acid + a strong base $\longrightarrow$ basic salt

The salt of a weak acid and a weak base may be acidic, neutral, or basic, depending on the relative strengths of the acids and bases involved.

The strong acids are HI, HBr, HCl, HNO_3, H_2SO_4, and $HClO_4$. The strong bases are the Group I and Group II hydroxides. Most others are considered weak.

Complete the chart. The first row is done for you.

Salt	Parent Acid	Acid Strength	Parent Base	Base Strength	Type of Salt
KBr	HBr	strong	KOH	strong	neutral
$Fe(NO_3)_2$					
NaF					
NH_4Cl					
$Ca(NO_3)_2$					
Li_3PO_4					
K_2SO_4					
AlI_3					
$MgCO_3$					
$Zn(ClO_4)_2$					

Conductors and Electrolytes

Pure metals are good conductors of electricity. **Electrolytes** are aqueous solutions that conduct electricity. Acids, bases, and salts (ionic compounds) are electrolytes. **Nonelectrolytes** are aqueous solutions that do not conduct electricity. The solutes used to form nonelectrolytes are covalently bonded.

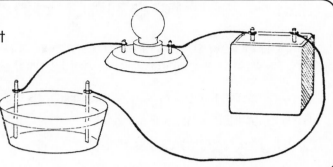

Identify each as a conductor or nonconductor by writing *C* or *N* next to each.

1. copper _____

2. hydrogen _____

3. NaOH(aq) _____

4. NaCl(s) _____

5. NaCl(aq) _____

6. magnesium _____

7. H_2SO_4 _____

8. NH_4OH _____

9. HCl(aq) _____

10. $Ca(OH)_2(aq)$ _____

11. $C_6H_{12}O_6$(aq) _____

12. CH_3OH _____

13. KNO_3(s) _____

14. KNO_3(aq) _____

15. chlorine _____

16. HNO_3 _____

17. $NaNO_3$(aq) _____

18. $C_{12}H_{22}O_{11}$ _____

19. C_2H_5OH _____

20. gold _____

Effect of Dissolved Particles on Freezing and Boiling Points

The graph below shows a time/temperature graph for the heating of water. Directly on the graph, sketch the approximate curve that would result when

    A. 5 g of sugar ($C_6H_{12}O_6$) are dissolved in the sample;

    B. 5 g of NaCl are dissolved;

    C. 10 g of NaCl are dissolved.

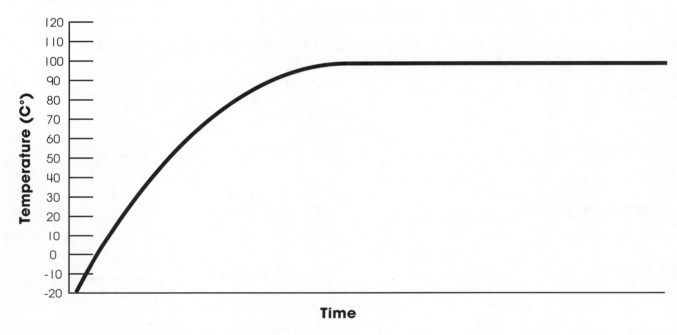

Do the same on the graph below for solutions A, B, and C when the solution is cooled through its freezing point.

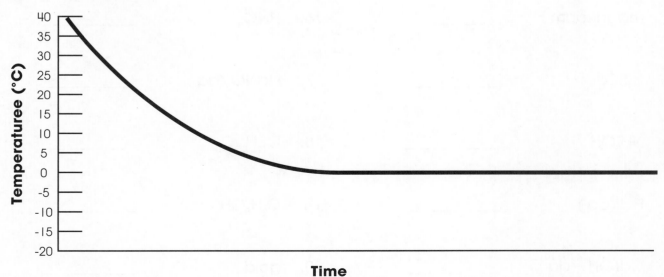

Concentration (Mass/Volume)

$$\text{concentration (in g/L)} = \frac{\text{mass of solute}}{\text{volume of solution}}$$

Solve each problem.

1. A sugar solution contains 26 g of sugar in 0.50 L of solution. What is the concentration?

2. 45 grams of salt are dissolved in 0.10 L of solution. What is the concentration in g/L?

3. A solution contains 25 g of sugar per L of solution. How many grams of sugar are in 1.5 L of solution?

4. A solution contains 85 g of corn syrup per L of solution. How many grams of corn syrup are in 500 mL of solution?

5. How many liters of salt solution would be needed to provide 30 g of salt if the concentration of the solution is 20 g/L?

Concentration (Percent by Volume)

$$\% \text{ volume} = \frac{V_{solute}}{V_{total}} \times 100\%$$

Solve each problem. Assume all volumes are additive.

1. To make 100 mL of solution, 25 mL of ethanol are added to water. Find the percent by volume of ethanol.

2. 50 mL of ethanol are added to 100 mL of water. What is the percent by volume of ethanol?

3. 3.0 L of antifreeze are added to 4.0 L of water. Find the percent by volume of antifreeze.

4. A popular fruit drink contains 5% by volume of fruit juice. How much fruit juice is in 500 mL of the fruit drink?

5. How much corn syrup should be added to water to make 200 mL of a 10% by-volume solution?

Concentration (Percent by Mass)

$$\text{concentration} = \frac{\text{mass of solute}}{\text{volume of solution}} \times 100\%$$

Solve each problem.

1.	What percent by mass of sugar will 25 g of sugar in 75 g of solution have?
2.	35 g of salt are dissolved in 500 g of total solution. What is the percent by mass of salt?
3.	50 g of sugar are dissolved in 100 g of water. What is the percent by mass of sugar?
4.	75 g of potassium nitrate are dissolved in 150 g of water. What is the percent by mass of potassium nitrate?
5.	How many grams of sodium bromide are in 200 g of a solution that is 15% sodium bromide by mass?

Solubility

Identify each compound as *soluble* or *insoluble,* following the rules for solubility.

1. $AgNO_3$ _____

2. K_2CO_3 _____

3. $Ca_3(PO_4)_2$ _____

4. $AgCl$ _____

5. $NaOH$ _____

6. NH_4Cl _____

7. KBr _____

8. $MgCO_3$ _____

9. FeS _____

10. $CuC_2H_3O_2$ _____

11. $(NH_4)_2SO_4$ _____

12. $Ca(OH)_2$ _____

13. Na_2SO_4 _____

14. $BaSO_4$ _____

15. KI _____

16. $(NH_4)_3PO_4$ _____

17. $Cu(NO_3)_2$ _____

18. $AlPO_4$ _____

19. $CaCO_3$ _____

20. $(NH_4)_2S$ _____

Name________________________________

Naming Organic Compounds

Name each organic compound.

1.

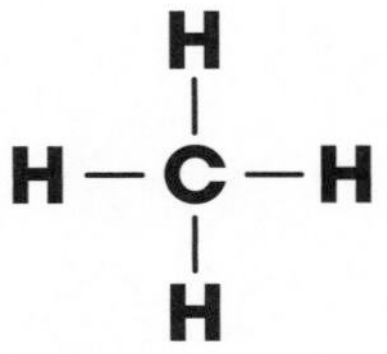

2.

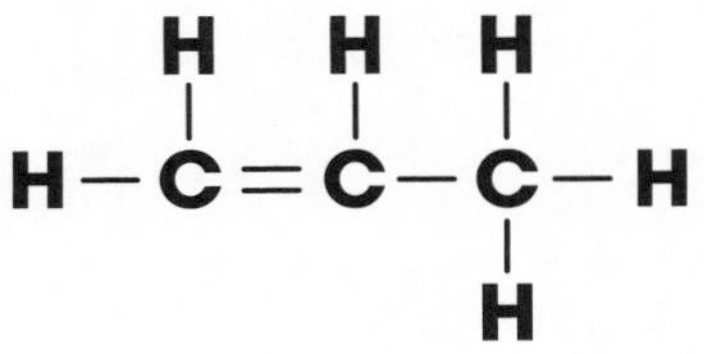

3.

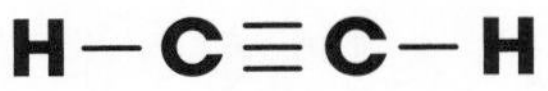

4.

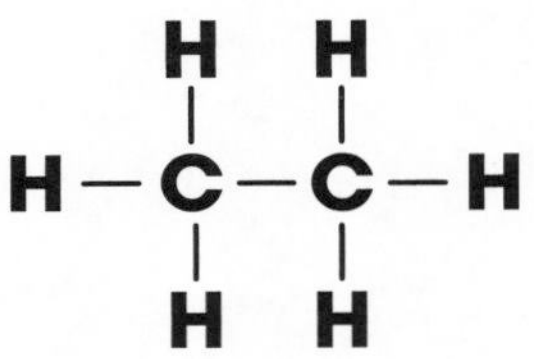

5.

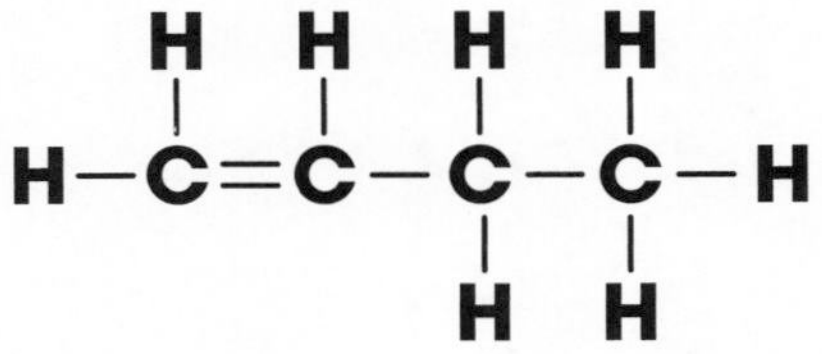

6.

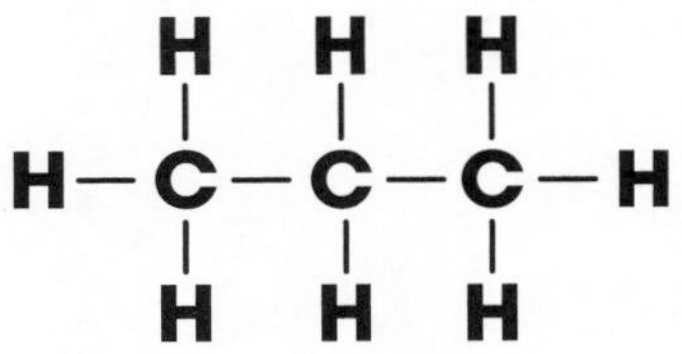

7.

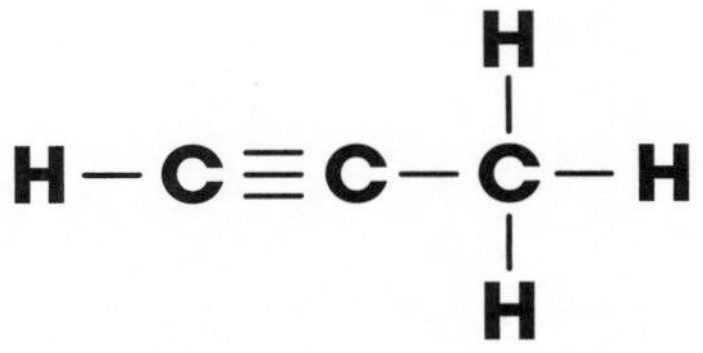

8.

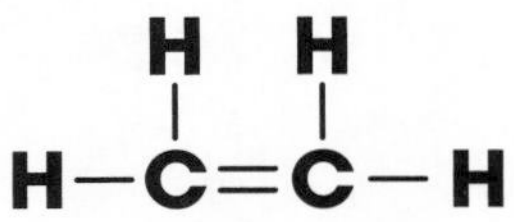

Name _____

Drawing Structural Formulas

Draw the structural formula for each compound.

1. ethane	5. propyne
2. propene	6. methane
3. l-butyne	7. ethyne
4. ethene	8. l-pentene

Isomers

Isomers have the same chemical formula but different structural formulas.

Match the structure with its isomer.

1. _____

$$H-\underset{\underset{H}{|}}{\overset{\overset{H}{|}}{C}}-\underset{\underset{H}{|}}{\overset{\overset{H}{|}}{C}}-\underset{\underset{H}{|}}{\overset{\overset{H}{|}}{C}}-OH$$

A.

$$H-\underset{\underset{H}{|}}{\overset{\overset{H}{|}}{C}}-\underset{\underset{H}{|}}{\overset{\overset{CH_3}{|}}{C}}-\underset{\underset{H}{|}}{\overset{\overset{H}{|}}{C}}-H$$

2. _____

$$H-\underset{\underset{H}{|}}{\overset{\overset{H}{|}}{C}}-\overset{\overset{O}{\|}}{C}-\underset{\underset{H}{|}}{\overset{\overset{H}{|}}{C}}-H$$

B.

$$H-\underset{\underset{H}{|}}{\overset{\overset{H}{|}}{C}}-\underset{\underset{H}{|}}{\overset{\overset{OH}{|}}{C}}-\underset{\underset{H}{|}}{\overset{\overset{H}{|}}{C}}-H$$

3. _____

$$H-\underset{\underset{H}{|}}{\overset{\overset{H}{|}}{C}}-\underset{\underset{H}{|}}{\overset{\overset{H}{|}}{C}}-\underset{\underset{H}{|}}{\overset{\overset{H}{|}}{C}}-\underset{\underset{H}{|}}{\overset{\overset{H}{|}}{C}}-H$$

C.

$$H_3C-\underset{\underset{CH_3}{|}}{\overset{\overset{CH_3}{|}}{C}}-CH_3$$

4. _____

$$H-\underset{\underset{H}{|}}{\overset{\overset{H}{|}}{C}}-\underset{\underset{H}{|}}{\overset{\overset{H}{|}}{C}}-\underset{\underset{H}{|}}{\overset{\overset{H}{|}}{C}}-\underset{\underset{H}{|}}{\overset{\overset{H}{|}}{C}}-\underset{\underset{H}{|}}{\overset{\overset{H}{|}}{C}}-H$$

D.

$$H-\underset{\underset{H}{|}}{\overset{\overset{H}{|}}{C}}-\underset{\underset{H}{|}}{\overset{\overset{H}{|}}{C}}-\overset{\overset{O}{\|}}{C}-H$$

5. _____

$$H-\underset{\underset{H}{|}}{\overset{\overset{H}{|}}{C}}-\overset{\overset{O}{\|}}{C}-OH$$

E.

$$H-\underset{\underset{H}{|}}{\overset{\overset{H}{|}}{C}}-O-\overset{\overset{O}{\|}}{C}-H$$

Organic Chemistry Crossword

Across

4. Compound containing only carbon and hydrogen

6. Produced when one or more of the hydrogens in a hydrocarbon is replaced by a hydroxyl group

7. Compound where all carbon atoms are joined by single covalent bonds

8. Sugar and starch

9. Long chains of carbon atoms produced by joining small chains together

10. Ingredient of gasoline

Down

1. Compounds with the same chemical formula but different structures

2. Organic compound in the body used to store energy

3. Compound containing a double or triple covalent bond

5. Polymer made from smaller molecules called amino acids

9. Mixture of hydrocarbons that is used for fuels

Answer Key

The Scientific Method

Arrange the steps of the scientific method in the proper order.

2 Research the problem.

5 Observe and record.

3 Make a hypothesis.

1 Identify the problem.

6 Arrive at a conclusion.

4 Test the hypothesis.

Match each term with the correct definition.

B 1. hypothesis

F 2. control

G 3. variable

A 4. experiment

D 5. conclusion

E 6. theory

C 7. data

A. organized process used to test a hypothesis

B. an educated guess about the solution to a problem

C. observations and measurements recorded during an experiment

D. a judgment based on the results of an experiment

E. a logical explanation for events that occur in nature

F. used to show that the result of an experiment is really due to the condition being tested

G. factor that changes in an experiment

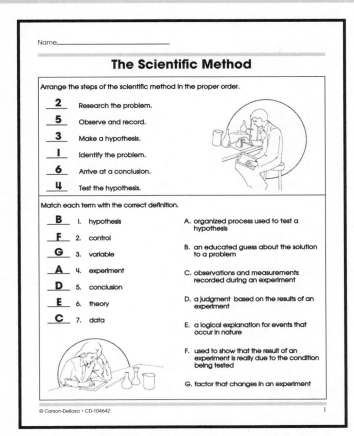

Safety in the Laboratory

Identify what is wrong in each laboratory situation.

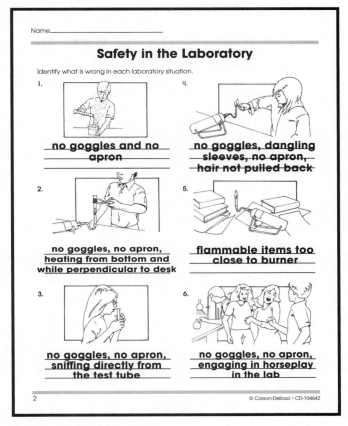

1. **no goggles and no apron**

4. **no goggles, dangling sleeves, no apron, hair not pulled back**

2. **no goggles, no apron, heating from bottom and while perpendicular to desk**

5. **flammable items too close to burner**

3. **no goggles, no apron, sniffing directly from the test tube**

6. **no goggles, no apron, engaging in horseplay in the lab**

Laboratory Equipment

Write the name of each lab instrument or piece of equipment.

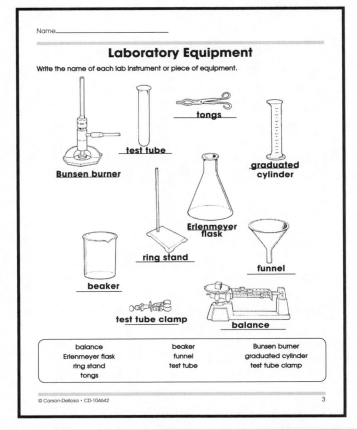

tongs

test tube

graduated cylinder

Bunsen burner

Erlenmeyer flask

ring stand

funnel

beaker

test tube clamp

balance

balance	beaker	Bunsen burner
Erlenmeyer flask	funnel	graduated cylinder
ring stand	test tube	test tube clamp
tongs		

Using the Balance

Identify the mass shown on each balance.

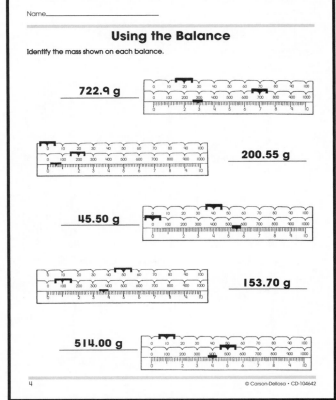

722.9 g

200.55 g

45.50 g

153.70 g

514.00 g

Answer Key

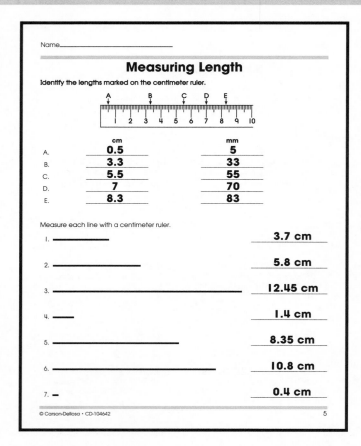

Measuring Length

Identify the lengths marked on the centimeter ruler.

	cm	mm
A.	0.5	5
B.	3.3	33
C.	5.5	55
D.	7	70
E.	8.3	83

Measure each line with a centimeter ruler.

1.	3.7 cm
2.	5.8 cm
3.	12.45 cm
4.	1.4 cm
5.	8.35 cm
6.	10.8 cm
7.	0.4 cm

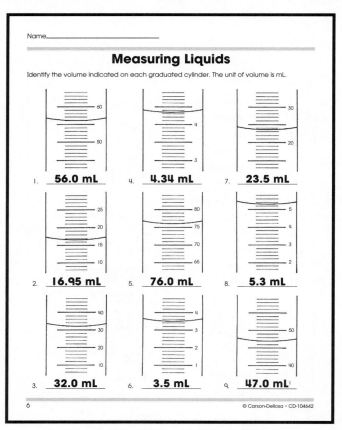

Measuring Liquids

Identify the volume indicated on each graduated cylinder. The unit of volume is mL.

1. 56.0 mL	4. 4.34 mL	7. 23.5 mL
2. 16.95 mL	5. 76.0 mL	8. 5.3 mL
3. 32.0 mL	6. 3.5 mL	9. 47.0 mL

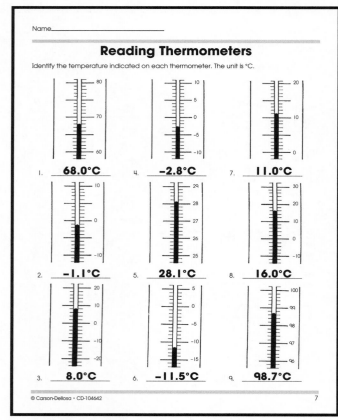

Reading Thermometers

Identify the temperature indicated on each thermometer. The unit is °C.

1. 68.0°C	4. –2.8°C	7. 11.0°C
2. –1.1°C	5. 28.1°C	8. 16.0°C
3. 8.0°C	6. –11.5°C	9. 98.7°C

Metrics and Measurement

Scientists use the metric system of measurement, which is based on the number 10. It is important to be able to convert from one unit to another.

kilo-	hecto-	deca-	Basic Units	deci-	centi-	milli-
(k)	(h)	(da)	gram (g)	(d)	(c)	(m)
1000	100	10	liter (L)	0.1	0.01	0.001
10^3	10^2	10^1	meter (m)	10^{-1}	10^{-2}	10^{-3}

Using the chart above, we can determine how many places to move the decimal point and in what direction by counting the places from one unit to the other.

Example: Convert 5 mL to L.

Answer: To go from milli (m) to the basic unit (liters), count on the above chart three places to the left. Move the decimal point three places to the left and 5 mL becomes 0.005 L.

Convert each measurement.

1. 35 mL =	0.35 dL	6. 4,500 mg =	4.5 g
2. 950 g =	0.950 kg	7. 25 cm =	250 mm
3. 275 mm =	27.5 cm	8. 0.005 kg =	0.5 dag
4. 1.0 L =	0.001 kL	9. 0.075 m =	7.5 cm
5. 1.0 mL =	0.001 L	10. 15 g =	15,000 mg

Answer Key

Name_____

Unit Conversions and Factor-Label Method

Another method of converting from one unit to another involves multiplying by a conversion factor. A **conversion factor** is a fraction that is equal to one. For example, 60 minutes is equal to 1 hour. Therefore, 60 min./1 hr. or 1 hr./60 min. = 1. When you multiply by the number 1, the value of the number is not changed, although the units may be different.

Example: How many milligrams are in 20 kilograms?
Use the following relationships:
1,000 mg = 1 g
1,000 g = 1 kg
1. Start with the original number and unit.
2. Multiply by a unit factor with the unit to be discarded on the bottom and the desired unit on top.
3. Cancel units.
4. Perform numerical calculations.

$$20 \text{ kg} \times \frac{1000 \text{ g}}{1 \text{ kg}} \times \frac{1000 \text{ mg}}{1 \text{ g}} = 20,000,000 \text{ or } 2 \times 10^7 \text{ mg}$$

Perform each conversion using unit factoring.

1.	500 mL =	**0.5** L	11.	4.2 L =	**4,200** mL
2.	25 cg =	**0.25** g	12.	0.35 km =	**350** m
3.	400 mg =	**0.0004** kg	13.	2.3 L =	**2,300** mL
4.	30 cm =	**300** mm	14.	4.5 yd. =	**162** In.
5.	3500 sec. =	**0.97** hr.	15.	50 mm =	**0.00005** km
6.	1.25 L =	**1,250** mL	16.	150 mg =	**0.15** g
7.	15 m =	**15,000** mm	17.	150 kg =	**150,000** g
8.	0.75 L =	**750** mL	18.	23 mL =	**0.023** L
9.	6.4 kg =	**6,400** g	19.	0.156 g =	**156** mg
10.	7,200 m =	**7.2** km	20.	2 yr. =	**63,072,000** sec.

(Assume 1 year = 365 days)

9

Name_____

Using Correct Units

For each of the following commonly used metric measurements, identify its symbol. Then, use the symbols to complete each sentence.

mL milliliter   **mg** milligram   **L** liter   **cm** centimeter
kg kilogram   **mm** millimeter   **km** kilometer   **g** gram
m meter   **ms** millisecond   **µg** microgram   **nm** nanometer

1. Colas may be purchased in one- or two- **L** bottles.
2. The mass of a bowling ball is 7.25 **kg** .
3. The length of the common housefly is about I **cm** .
4. The mass of a paper clip is about 1 **g** .
5. One teaspoon of cough syrup has a volume of 5 **mL** .
6. The speed limit on the highway is usually 106.6 **km** /h or 29.6 **m** /s.
7. The length of the small intestine in a man is about 6.25 **m** .
8. Viruses such as AIDS, polio, and flu range in length from 17 to 1,000 **nm** .
9. Adults require at least 1,000 **mg** of calcium to meet the US RDA.
10. In a vacuum, light can travel 300 km in 1 **ms** .
11. The mass of a proton is 1.67 x 10⁻¹⁸ **µg** .
12. Blue light has a wavelength of about 500 **nm** .
13. One mole of oxygen gas at STP occupies 22.4 **L** .
14. Myoglobin, a protein that stores oxygen, has a mass of 2.98 x 10⁻¹⁴ **µg** .
15. Buttery popcorn contained in a large 1- **L** bowl has a mass of about 50 **g** of fat and about 650 calories.
16. The dying comet fragments that continue to batter Jupiter travel at speeds of about 58,117 **km** / **s** , or 130,000 miles per hour.
17. The human heart has a mass of about 1.05 **kg** .
18. Stand with your arms raised out to your side. The distance from your nose to your outstretched middle finger is about 1 **m** .
19. The body mass of a flea is about 0.5 **mg** , and it can jump about 20 **cm** high.
20. On a statistical basis, smoking a single cigarette lowers your life expectancy by 642,000 **ms** , or 10.7 minutes.

10

Name_____

Scientific Notation

Scientists very often deal with very small and very large numbers, which can lead to a lot of confusion when counting zeros. We can express these numbers as powers of 10 so they are easier to read and understand.

Scientific notation takes the form of $M \times 10^n$ where $1 \le M < $ and n represents the number of decimal places to be moved. Positive n indicates the standard form is larger than zero, whereas negative n would indicate a number smaller than zero.

Example: Convert 1,500,000 to scientific notation.
Move the decimal point so that there is only one digit to its left, a total of 6 places.
$1,500,000 = 1.5 \times 10^6$

Example: Convert 0.00025 to scientific notation.
Move the decimal point 4 places to the right.
$0.00025 = 2.5 \times 10^{-4}$

(Note that when a number starts out less than one, the exponent is always negative.)

Convert each number to scientific notation.

1.	0.005 =	5×10^{-3}	6.	0.25 =	2.5×10^{-1}
2.	5,050 =	5.05×10^3	7.	0.025 =	2.5×10^{-2}
3.	0.0008 =	8×10^{-4}	8.	0.0025 =	2.5×10^{-3}
4.	1,000 =	1×10^3	9.	500 =	5×10^2
5.	1,000,000 =	1×10^6	10.	5,000 =	5×10^3

Convert each number to standard notation.

11.	1.5×10^3 =	**1,500**	16.	3.35×10^{-1} =	**0.335**
12.	1.5×10^{-3} =	**0.0015**	17.	1.2×10^{-4} =	**0.00012**
13.	3.75×10^{-2} =	**0.0375**	18.	1×10^4 =	**10,000**
14.	3.75×10^2 =	**375**	19.	1×10^{-1} =	**0.1**
15.	2.2×10^5 =	**220,000**	20.	4×10^0 =	**4**

11

Name_____

Calculations Using Significant Figures

When multiplying numbers in scientific notation, multiply the first part of the number, the **mantissa**, and add the exponents.

Example: $(3.0 \times 10^2)(2.5 \times 10^6) = $
Multiply: $3.0 \times 2.5 = 7.5$
Then, add: $2 + 6 = 8$
$= 7.5 \times 10^8$

When dividing numbers in scientific notation, divide the mantissa and subtract the exponents.

Example: $\frac{9.0 \times 10^6}{4.5 \times 10^2}$
Divide: 9.0 by 4.5 = 2.0
Then, subtract: $2 - 6 = 4$
$= 2.0 \times 10^4$

Perform each calculation. Express all answers in scientific notation.

1. $(1.5 \times 10^3)(3.5 \times 10^5)$ **5.25×10^8**	6. $(4 \times 10^5) \div (1 \times 10^{-3})$ **4×10^8**
2. $(2.0 \times 10^5)(2.0 \times 10^9)$ **4.0×10^{14}**	7. $(7.6 \times 10^{-3})(8.2 \times 10^{-4})$ **6.2×10^{-7}**
3. $(6.2 \times 10^6) \div (3.1 \times 10^2)$ **2.0×10^4**	8. $(8.5 \times 10^9) \div (2.5 \times 10^5)$ **3.4×10^{-5}**
4. $(5.0 \times 10^4) \div (2.5 \times 10^3)$ **2.0×10**	9. $(7.0 \times 10^{11})(7.0 \times 10^{-11})$ **4.9×10**
5. $(6.8 \times 10^7)(2.2 \times 10^{-5})$ **1.5×10^2**	10. $(1.3 \times 10^9) \div (2.6 \times 10^5)$ **5.0×10^4**

12

Answer Key

Density

Name_____

Which has the greater mass, air or lead? Most would answer lead, but this question actually does not have an answer. To compare these two things, you need to know how much of each you have. A large amount of air could have a greater mass than a small amount of lead. To compare different things, we have to compare the masses of each that occupy the same space, or volume. This is called **density**. It is measured in units of g/mL or g/cm³.

$$density = \frac{mass}{volume} \quad or \quad D = \frac{M}{V}$$

Solve each problem.

1. What is the density of carbon dioxide gas if 0.196 g occupies a volume of 100 mL?
   1.96×10^{-3} g/mL

2. A block of wood that measures 3.0 cm on each side has a mass of 27 g. What is the density of the block?
   1.0 g/cm³

3. An irregularly shaped stone was lowered into a graduated cylinder holding a volume of water equal to 2.0 mL. The height of the water rose to 7.0 mL. If the mass of the stone was 25 g, what was its density?
   5.0 g/mL

4. A 10.0 cm³ sample of copper has a mass of 89.6 g. What is the density of copper?
   8.96 g/cm³

5. Silver has a density of 10.5 g/cm³, and gold has a density of 19.3 g/cm³. Which would have a greater mass, 5 cm³ of silver or 5 cm³ of gold?
   gold

6. Five mL of ethanol has a mass of 3.9 g , and 5.0 mL of benzene has a mass of 4.4 g. Which liquid is denser?
   benzene

7. A sample of iron in the shape of a rectangular prism has the dimensions of 2 cm × 3 cm × 2 cm. If the mass of this object is 94 g, what is the density of iron?
   7.83 g/cm³

Graphing of Data

Name_____

Graphing is an important tool in science. It enables us to see trends that are not always obvious. Graph the following data and answer the questions below.

Mass of Liquid (g)	Volume of Liquid (cm³)
20	4
100	20
75	15
40	8
10	2

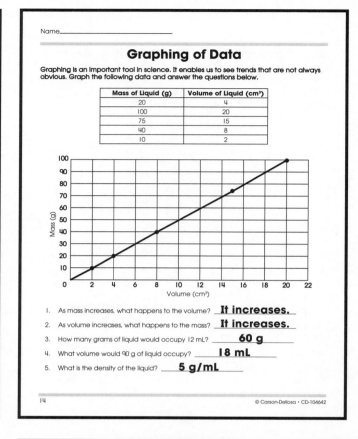

1. As mass increases, what happens to the volume? **It increases.**
2. As volume increases, what happens to the mass? **It increases.**
3. How many grams of liquid would occupy 12 mL? **60 g**
4. What volume would 90 g of liquid occupy? **18 mL**
5. What is the density of the liquid? **5 g/mL**

Determining Speed (Velocity)

Name_____

Speed is a measure of how fast an object is moving or traveling. **Velocity** is a measure of how fast an object is traveling in a certain direction. Both speed and velocity include the distance traveled compared to the amount of time taken to cover this distance.

$$speed = \frac{distance}{time} \qquad velocity = \frac{distance}{time} \text{ in a specific direction}$$

Solve each problem.

1. What is the velocity of a car that traveled a total of 75 kilometers north in 1.5 hours?
   50 km/h

2. What is the velocity of a plane that traveled 3,000 miles from New York to California in 5.0 hours? **600 mi/h**

3. John took 45 minutes to bicycle to his grandmother's house, a total of four kilometers. What was his velocity in km/h? **5.3 km/h**

4. It took 3.5 hours for a train to travel the distance between two cities at a velocity of 120 miles/h. How many miles lie between the two cities?
   420 mi.

5. How long would it take for a car to travel a distance of 200 kilometers if it is traveling at a velocity of 55 km/h? **3.6 h**

6. A car is traveling at 100 km/h. How many hours will it take to cover a distance of 750 km? **7.5 h**

7. A plane traveled for about 2.5 hours at a velocity of 1,200 km/h. What distance did it travel? **3,000 km**

8. A girl is pedaling her bicycle at a velocity of 0.10 km/min. How far will she travel in two hours? **12 km**

9. An ant carries food at a speed of 1 cm/s. How long will it take the ant to carry a cookie crumb from the kitchen table to the ant hill, a distance of 50 m? Express your answer in seconds, minutes, and hours. **5,000 s; 83.3 min.; 1.39 h**

10. The water in the Buffalo River flows at an average speed of 5 km/h. If you and a friend decide to canoe 16 kilometers down the river, how many hours and minutes will it take? **3 h, 12 min.**

Calculating Average Speed

Name_____

Graph the following data and answer the questions below.

Time (min.)	Distance (m)
0	0
1	50
2	75
3	90
4	110
5	125

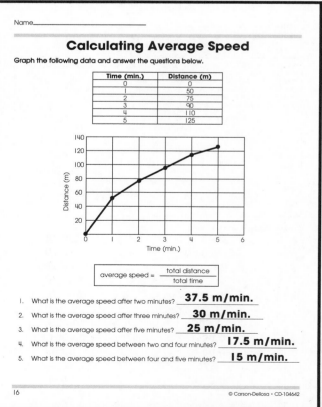

$$average\ speed = \frac{total\ distance}{total\ time}$$

1. What is the average speed after two minutes? **37.5 m/min.**
2. What is the average speed after three minutes? **30 m/min.**
3. What is the average speed after five minutes? **25 m/min.**
4. What is the average speed between two and four minutes? **17.5 m/min.**
5. What is the average speed between four and five minutes? **15 m/min.**

Answer Key

Acceleration Calculations

Acceleration means a change in speed or direction. It can also be defined as a change in velocity per unit of time. It is measured in units such as km/h/s and m/s/s (m/s²).

$$a = \frac{v_f - v_i}{t}$$

where a = acceleration
v_f = final velocity
v_i = initial velocity
t = time

Calculate the acceleration for the following data.

	Initial Velocity	Final Velocity	Time	Acceleration
1.	0 km/h	24 km/h	3 s	**8 km/h/s**
2.	0 m/s	35 m/s	5 s	**7 m/s²**
3.	20 km/h	60 km/h	10 s	**4 km/h/s**
4.	50 m/s	150 m/s	5 s	**20 m/s²**
5.	25 km/h	1,200 km/h	2 min.	**587.5 km/h/min.**

6. A car accelerates from a standstill to 60 km/h in 10.0 seconds.

   What is its acceleration? **6 km/h/s**

7. A car accelerates from 25 km/h to 55 km/h in 30 seconds.

   What is its acceleration? **1 km/h/s**

8. A train is accelerating at a rate of 2.0 km/h/s. Its initial velocity is 20 km/h.

   What is its velocity after 30 seconds? **80 km/h**

9. A runner achieves a velocity of 11.1 m/s 9 seconds after he begins.

   What is his acceleration? **1.2 m/s²**

© Carson-Dellosa • CD-104642   17

Graphing Speed vs. Time

Graph the following data and answer the questions below.

Speed (km/h)	Time (s)
0.0	0
10.0	2
20.0	4
30.0	6
40.0	8
50.0	10

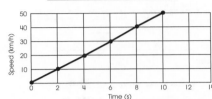

1. As time increases, what happens to the speed? **It increases.**

2. What is the speed at 5 s? **25 km/h**

3. Assuming constant acceleration, what would be the speed at 14 s? **70 km/h**

4. At what time would the object reach a speed of 45 km/h? **9 s**

5. What is the object's acceleration? **5 km/h/s**

6. What would the shape of the graph be if a speed of 50.0 km/h is maintained from 10 s to 20 s? **a horizontal line**

7. Based on the information in problem 6, calculate the acceleration from 10 s to 20 s. **0 km/h/s**

8. What would the shape of the graph be if the speed of the object decreased from 50.0 km/h at 20 s to 30 km/h at 40 s? **a line sloping down from left to right**

9. What is the acceleration in problem 8? **–1 km/h/s**

18   © Carson-Dellosa • CD-104642

Graphing Distance vs. Time

Graph the following data and answer the questions below.

Distance (km)	Time (s)
0	0
5	10
12	20
20	30
30	40
42	50
56	60

1. What is the average speed at 20 s? **0.6 km/s**

2. What is the average speed at 30 s? **0.67 km/s**

3. What is the acceleration between 20 s and 30 s? **0.007 km/s/s**

4. What is the average speed at 40 s? **0.75 km/s**

5. What is the average speed at 60 s? **0.93 km/s**

6. What is the acceleration between 40 s and 60 s? **0.009 km/s/s**

7. Is the object accelerating at a constant rate? **no**

© Carson-Dellosa • CD-104642   19

Gravity and Acceleration

The acceleration of a freely falling body is 9.8 m/s/s (or 9.8 m/s²) due to the force of gravity.

Using the formula $a = \frac{v_f - v_i}{t}$, we can calculate the velocity of a falling object at any time if the initial velocity is known.

Example: What is the velocity of a rubber ball dropped from a building roof after 5 seconds?

$$9.8 \text{ m/s}^2 = \frac{v_f - 0}{5 \text{ s}}$$
$$v_f = 49 \text{ m/s}$$

Solve each problem.

1. What is the velocity of a quarter dropped from a tower after 10 s?

   98 m/s

2. If a block of wood dropped from a tall building has attained a velocity of 78.4 m/s, how long has it been falling?

   8 s

3. If a ball that is freely falling has attained a velocity of 19.6 m/s after 2 s, what is its velocity 5 s later?

   68.6 m/s

4. A piece of metal has attained a velocity of 107.8 m/s after falling for 10 s. What is its initial velocity?

   9.8 m/s

5. How long will it take an object that falls from rest to attain a velocity of 147 m/s?

   15 s

20   © Carson-Dellosa • CD-104642

Answer Key

Gravity, Acceleration, and Distance

The distance covered by a freely falling body is calculated by the following formula:

$$d = \frac{at^2}{2}$$

where d = distance
a = acceleration
t = time

Example: How far will an object fall in 5 seconds?

$$d = \frac{(9.8 \text{ m/s}^2)(5 \text{ s})^2}{2} = 122.5 \text{ m}$$

Example: What is the average velocity of a ball that attains a velocity of 39.2 m/s after 4 seconds?

$$v_a = \frac{v_f - v_i}{2} = \frac{39.2 - 0}{2} = 19.6 \text{ m/s}$$

Solve each problem.

1. How far will a rubber ball fall in 10 s? __**490 m**__

2. How far will a rubber ball fall in 20 s? __**1,960 m**__

3. How long will it take an object dropped from a window to fall a distance of 78.4 m? __**4 s**__

4. What is the final velocity of the ball in problem 1? __**98 m/s**__

5. What is the average velocity of the ball in problem 1? __**49 m/s**__

6. An airplane is traveling at an altitude of 31,360 m. A box of supplies is dropped from its cargo hold. How long will it take to reach the ground? __**80 s**__

7. At what velocity will the box in problem 6 be traveling when it hits the ground? __**784 m/s**__

8. What is the average velocity of the box in problem 6? __**392 m/s**__

21

Force Diagrams

Find the resultant force in each diagram and draw the resultant vector. Use a ruler and a protractor where necessary. Scale: 1 cm = 10 N, where *N* represents newtons of force.

1. 20 N → → 30 N   **10 N** →

4. ← 20 N ← 30 N   **50 N** ←

2. **42 N** 30 N 30 N

5. **55 N** 30 N 30 N

3. **30 N** 30 N 12 N 135° 30 N

6. **40 N** 30 N 15 N 157.5° 30 N

22

Force and Acceleration

A **force** is a push or a pull. To calculate force, we use the following formula:

$$F = ma$$

where F = force (N)
m = mass (kg)
a = acceleration (m/s²)

Example: With what force will a rubber ball hit the ground if it has a mass of 0.25 kg?

$$F = (0.25 \text{ kg})(9.8 \text{ m/s}^2)$$
$$F = 2.45 \text{ N}$$

Solve each problem.

1. With what force will a car hit a tree if the car has a mass of 3,000 kg and it is accelerating at a rate of 2 m/s²?

   6,000 N

2. A 10-kg bowling ball would require what force to accelerate it down an alleyway at a rate of 3 m/s²?

   30 N

3. What is the mass of a falling rock if it hits the ground with a force of 147 N?

   15 kg

4. What is the acceleration of a softball if it has a mass of 0.50 kg and hits the catcher's glove with a force of 25 N?

   50 m/s²

5. What is the mass of a truck if it is accelerating at a rate of 5 m/s² and hits a parked car with a force of 14,000 N?

   2,800 kg

23

Motion Matching

Match the term with its definition.

1. __**G**__ kinetic
2. __**J**__ centripetal
3. __**A**__ mass
4. __**D**__ acceleration
5. __**E**__ velocity
6. __**B**__ weight
7. __**K**__ gravity
8. __**H**__ inertia
9. __**C**__ speed
10. __**I**__ momentum
11. __**F**__ newton

A. amount of matter in an object
B. amount of force exerted on an object due to gravity
C. distance covered per unit of time
D. rate at which velocity changes over time
E. speed in a given direction
F. unit of measurement for force
G. energy of motion
H. tendency of a moving object to keep moving
I. depends on the mass and velocity of an object
J. type of force that keeps objects moving in a circle
K. attractive force between two objects

24

Answer Key

Name_____

Heat Calculations

Heat is measured in units of joules (J) or calories (cal). The amount of heat given off or absorbed can be calculated by the following formula:

$$\Delta Q = m \times \Delta T \times C$$
heat = (mass in grams)(change in temperature)(specific heat)

The specific heat of water is **1.0 cal/g °C or 4.2 J/g °C.**

Solve each problem.

1. How many calories are absorbed by a pot of water with a mass of 500 g in order to raise the temperature from 20°C to 30°C?

   5,000 cal

2. How many joules would be absorbed for the water in problem 1?

   21,000 J

3. If the specific heat of iron is 0.46 J/g C°, how much heat is needed to warm 50 g of iron from 20°C to 100°C?

   1,840 J

4. If it takes 105 calories to warm 100 g of aluminum from 20°C to 25°C, what is the specific heat of aluminum?

   0.21 cal/g °C

5. If it takes 31,500 J of heat to warm 750 g of water, what was the temperature change?

   10°C

Name_____

Heat and Phase Changes

During a phase change, the temperature remains the same. For these calculations, use the following formulas:

For freezing and melting, heat = (mass in grams)(heat of fusion)
For boiling and condensing, heat = (mass in grams)(heat of vaporization)

The heat of fusion of water is 340 J/g.
The heat of vaporization of water is 2,300 J/g.

Solve each problem.

1. How many joules of heat are necessary to melt 500 g of ice at its freezing point?

   1.7×10^5 J

2. How many kilojoules is this?

   170 kJ

3. How much heat is necessary to vaporize 500 g of water at its boiling point?

   1.15×10^6 K

4. If 5,100 J of heat are given off when a sample of water freezes, what is the mass of the water?

   15 g

5. If 57,500 J of heat are given off when a sample of steam condenses, what is the mass of the steam?

   25 g

Name_____

Simple Machines

Identify the type of simple machine shown in each picture.

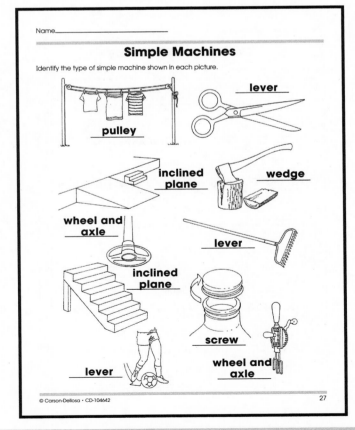

pulley

lever

inclined plane

wedge

wheel and axle

lever

inclined plane

screw

lever

wheel and axle

Name_____

Types of Levers

Classify each lever as *first*, *second*, or *third class*.

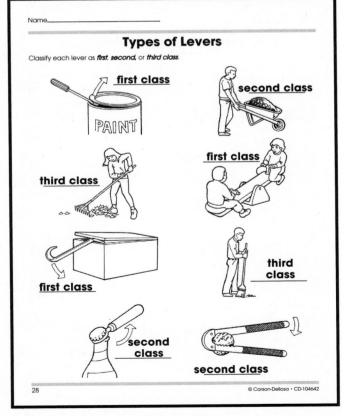

first class

second class

third class

first class

first class

third class

second class

second class

Answer Key

Potential and Kinetic Energy

Potential energy is stored energy due to position. **Kinetic energy** is energy that depends on mass and velocity (movement).

For a closed system, the sum of the potential energy and the kinetic energy is a constant. As the potential energy decreases, the kinetic energy increases.

potential energy = weight × height (P.E. = $w \times h$)

kinetic energy = $\frac{1}{2}$ mass × velocity² (K.E. = $\frac{1}{2} mv^2$)

units used:
energy = joules (J)
weight = newtons (N)
height = meters (m)
mass = kilograms (kg)
velocity = meters per second (m/s)

Solve each problem.

1. What is the potential energy of a rock that weighs 100 N that is sitting on top of a hill 300 m high?

   30,000 J

2. What is the kinetic energy of a bicycle with a mass of 14 kg traveling at a velocity of 3 m/s?

   63 J

3. A flower pot weighing 3 N is sitting on a windowsill 30 m from the ground. Is the energy of the flower pot potential or kinetic? How much energy does it possess?

   potential; 90 J

4. When the flower pot in problem 3 is only 10 m from the ground, what is its potential energy?

   30 J

5. How much of the total energy in problems 3 and 4 has been transformed to kinetic energy?

   60 J

6. A 1,200-kg automobile is traveling at a velocity of 100 m/s. Is its energy potential or kinetic? How much energy does it possess?

   kinetic; 6 × 10⁶ J

Calculating Work

Work has a special meaning in science. It is the product of the force applied to an object and the distance the object moves. The unit of work is the joule (J).

work = force (N) × distance (m)
W = $F \times D$

Solve each problem.

1. A book weighing 1.0 N is lifted 2 m. How much work was done?

   2 J

2. A force of 15 N is used to push a box along the floor a distance of 3 m. How much work was done?

   45 J

3. It took 50 J to push a chair 5 m across the floor. With what force was the chair pushed?

   10 N

4. A force of 100 N was necessary to lift a rock. A total of 150 J of work was done. How far was the rock lifted?

   1.5 m

5. It took 500 N of force to push a car 4 m. How much work was done?

   2,000 J

6. A young man exerted a force of 9,000 N on a stalled car but was unable to move it. How much work was done?

   0 J

Mechanical Advantage

$$MA = \frac{F_R}{F_E}$$

where F_R = resistance force
F_E = effort force

Identify the mechanical advantage of each simple machine.

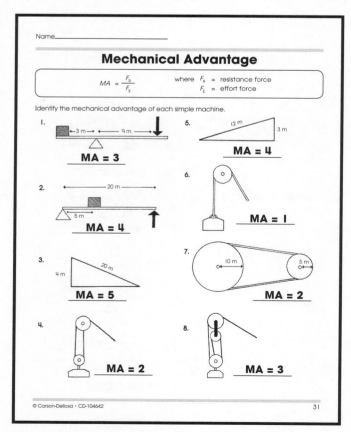

1. MA = 3

5. MA = 4

2. MA = 4

6. MA = 1

3. MA = 5

7. MA = 2

4. MA = 2

8. MA = 3

Calculating Efficiency

The amount of work obtained from a machine is always less than the amount of work put into it. This is because some of the work is lost due to friction. The efficiency of a machine can be calculated using the following formula.

$$\text{percent efficiency} = \frac{\text{work output}}{\text{work input}} \times 100$$

Find the efficiency of each machine.

1. A man expends 100 J of work to move a box up an inclined plane. The amount of work produced is 80 J.

   80%

2. A box weighing 100 N is pushed up an inclined plane that is 5 m long. It takes a force of 75 N to push it to the top, which has a height of 3 m.

   80%

3. Using a lever, a person applies 60 N of force and moves the lever 1 m. This moves a 200-newton rock at the other end by 0.2 m.

   67%

4. A person in a wheelchair exerts a force of 25 N to go up a ramp that is 10 m long. The weight of the person and wheelchair is 60 N and the height of the ramp is 3 m.

   36%

5. A boy pushes a lever down 2 m with a force of 75 N. The box at the other end, with a weight of 50 N, moves up 2.5 m.

   83%

6. A pulley system operates with 40% efficiency. If the work put in is 200 J, how much useful work is produced?

   80 J

Answer Key

Calculating Power

Power is the amount of work done per unit of time. The unit for power, joules/second, is the watt.

$$power = \frac{work}{time}$$

work = joules (J)
time = seconds (s)

Solve each problem.

1. A set of pulleys is used to lift a piano weighing 1,000 N. The piano is lifted 3 m in 60 s. How much power is used?

50 W

2. How much power is used if a force of 35 N is used to push a box a distance of 10 m in 5 s?

70 W

3. What is the power of a kitchen blender if it can perform 3,750 J of work in 15 s?

250 W

4. How much work is done using a 500-watt microwave oven for 5 minutes?

150,000 J

5. How much work is done using a 60-watt lightbulb for 1 hour?

216,000 J

Force and Work Crossword

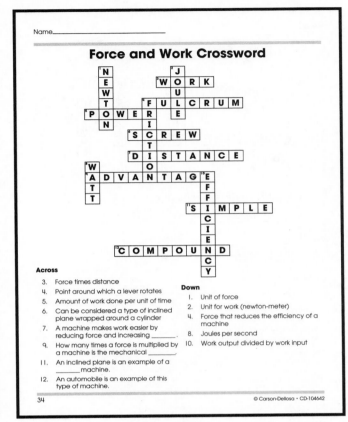

Across

3. Force times distance
4. Point around which a lever rotates
5. Amount of work done per unit of time
6. Can be considered a type of inclined plane wrapped around a cylinder
7. A machine makes work easier by reducing force and increasing _____.
9. How many times a force is multiplied by a machine is the mechanical _____.
11. An inclined plane is an example of a _____ machine.
12. An automobile is an example of this type of machine.

Down

1. Unit of force
2. Unit for work (newton-meter)
4. Force that reduces the efficiency of a machine
8. Joules per second
10. Work output divided by work input

Wave Diagram

Label the diagram with the following terms: *amplitude, wavelength, crest, trough,* and *rest position.*

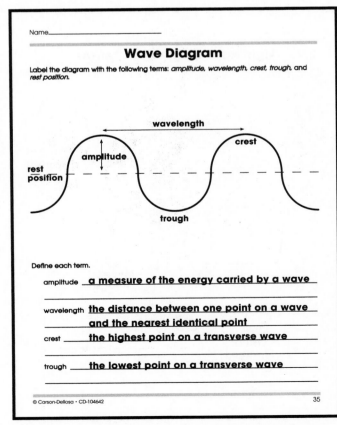

Define each term.

amplitude __a measure of the energy carried by a wave__

wavelength __the distance between one point on a wave and the nearest identical point__

crest __the highest point on a transverse wave__

trough __the lowest point on a transverse wave__

Wave Velocity Calculations

velocity (m/s) = wavelength (m) × frequency (Hz)

Solve each problem.

1. A tuning fork has a frequency of 280 hertz (Hz), and the wavelength of the sound produced is 1.5 m. Calculate the velocity of the wave.

420 m/s

2. A wave is moving toward shore with a velocity of 5.0 m/s. If its frequency is 2.5 Hz, what is its wavelength?

2.0 m

3. The speed of light is about 3.0×10^8 m/s. Red light has a wavelength of about 6.5×10^{-7} m. What is its frequency?

4.6×10^{14} Hz

4. The frequency of violet light is 7.5×10^{14} Hz. What is its wavelength?

4×10^{-7} m

5. A jump rope is shaken, producing a wave with a wavelength of 0.5 m. The crest of the wave passes a certain point 4 times per second. What is the velocity of the wave?

2 m/s

Answer Key

Name_____

Sound and Music Crossword

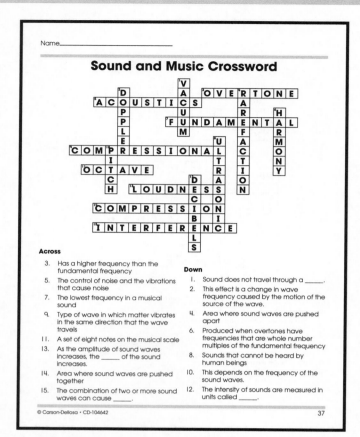

Across

3. Has a higher frequency than the fundamental frequency
5. The control of noise and the vibrations that cause noise
7. The lowest frequency in a musical sound
9. Type of wave in which matter vibrates in the same direction that the wave travels
11. A set of eight notes on the musical scale
13. As the amplitude of sound waves increases, the _____ of the sound increases.
14. Area where sound waves are pushed together
15. The combination of two or more sound waves can cause _____.

Down

1. Sound does not travel through a _____.
2. This effect is a change in wave frequency caused by the motion of the source of the wave.
4. Area where sound waves are pushed apart
6. Produced when overtones have frequencies that are whole number multiples of the fundamental frequency
8. Sounds that cannot be heard by human beings
10. This depends on the frequency of the sound waves.
12. The intensity of sounds are measured in units called _____.

© Carson-Dellosa • CD-104642   37

Name_____

Reflection

Draw the expected path of the light ray as it reflects off each mirror.

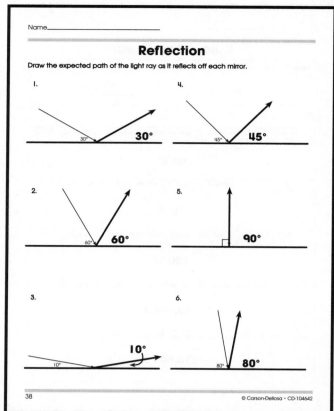

38   © Carson-Dellosa • CD-104642

Name_____

Refraction

Draw the pathway of the light beam as it passes through each substance. Using a protractor, measure the refracted angle.

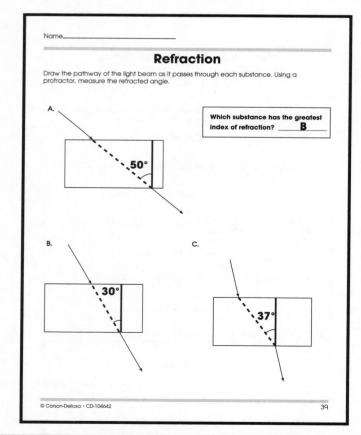

Which substance has the greatest index of refraction? ___B___

© Carson-Dellosa • CD-104642   39

Name_____

Light Rays and Convex Lenses

Draw the pathway of the light from the object on the left through the convex lense. Label the focal point and the inverted image.

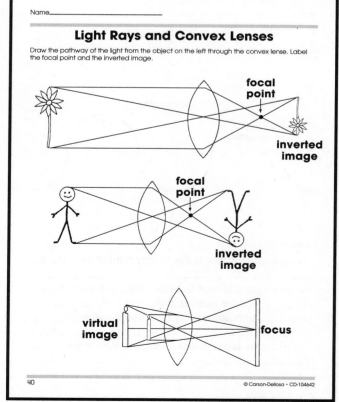

40   © Carson-Dellosa • CD-104642

Answer Key

Name_____

Light Rays and Concave Lenses

Draw the pathway of the light from the object on the left through the concave lens. Label the image and the focal point.

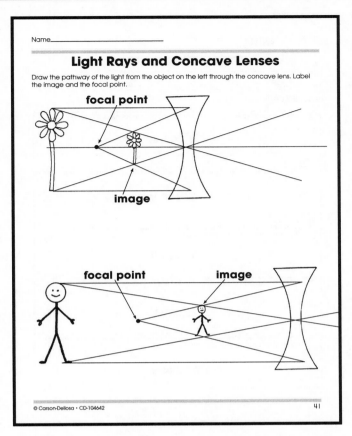

41

Name_____

White Light Spectrum

Label the colors coming through the prism as the white light is reflected through it.

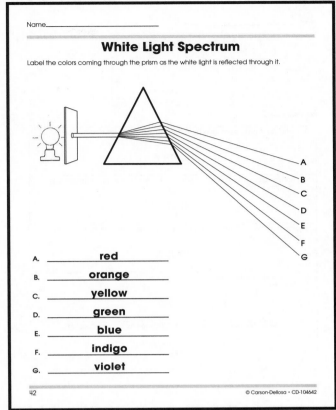

A. _____ red _____

B. _____ orange _____

C. _____ yellow _____

D. _____ green _____

E. _____ blue _____

F. _____ indigo _____

G. _____ violet _____

42

Name_____

Light Matching

Match the word with the correct definition or corresponding phrase.

1. __J__ hertz
2. __G__ wave velocity
3. __D__ frequency
4. __K__ reflection
5. __M__ wavelength
6. __B__ refraction
7. __O__ crest
8. __H__ trough
9. __N__ photon
10. __I__ light
11. __F__ prism
12. __E__ index of refraction
13. __P__ angle of incidence
14. __A__ angle of reflection
15. __L__ visible light spectrum
16. __C__ normal

A. the angle at which a ray "bounces off" of a surface

B. bending of light waves when they pass through another substance

C. an imaginary line drawn at a right angle to the surface of a barrier

D. number of waves that pass a given point in one second

E. tells how much a ray of light will bend as it travels through a given material

F. translucent material that separates white light into colors

G. frequency times wavelength

H. lowest part of a wave

I. type of electromagnetic radiation

J. unit for frequency

K. the bouncing of a wave off another object

L. a continuous band of colors arranged according to wavelength or frequency

M. distance between corresponding points on two waves

N. a particle of light

O. highest point of a wave

P. the angle at which a ray of light strikes a surface

43

Name_____

Magnetic Fields

Draw the pattern of magnetic fields around each magnet.

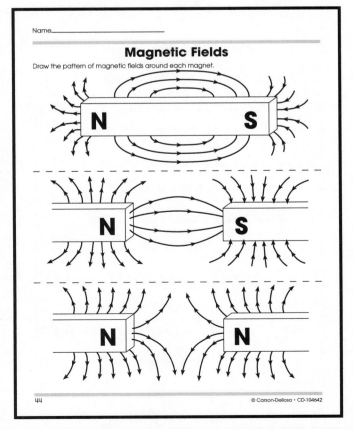

44

Answer Key

Name_____

Calculating Current

Ohm's Law states that $I = \dfrac{V}{R}$

where I = current (amperes, A)
         V = voltage (volts, V)
         R = resistance (ohms, Ω)

Solve each problem.

1. What is the current produced with a 9-volt battery through a resistance of 100 ohms?

   0.09 A

2. Find the current when a 12-volt battery is connected through a resistance of 25 ohms.

   0.48 A

3. If the potential difference is 120 V and the resistance is 50 ohms, what is the current?

   2.4 A

4. What would be the current in problem 3 if the potential difference were doubled?

   4.8 A

5. What would be the current in problem 3 if the resistance were doubled?

   1.2 A

Name_____

Calculating Voltage

V	=	I	×	R
voltage (volts, V)	=	current (amperes, A)	×	Resistance (ohms, Ω)

Solve each problem.

1. What voltage produces a current of 50 A with a resistance of 20 ohms?

   1,000 V

2. Silver has a resistance of 1.98×10^{-4} ohms. What voltage would produce a current of 100 A?

   0.0198 V

3. A current of 250 A is flowing through a copper wire with a resistance of 2.09×10^{-4} ohms. What is the voltage?

   0.0523 V

4. What voltage produces a current of 500 A with a resistance of 50 ohms?

   25,000 V

5. What voltage would produce a current of 100 A through an aluminum wire that has a resistance of 3.44×10^{-4} ohms?

   0.0344 V

Name_____

Calculating Resistance

$R = \dfrac{V}{I}$	resistance (ohms) =	$\dfrac{\text{voltage (V)}}{\text{current (A)}}$

Solve each problem.

1. What resistance would produce a current of 200 A with a potential difference of 2,000 V?

   10 ohms

2. A 12-volt battery produces a current of 25 A. What is the resistance?

   0.48 ohms

3. A 9-volt battery produces a current of 2.0 A. What is the resistance?

   4.5 ohms

4. An overhead wire has a potential difference of 2,000 V. If the current flowing through the wire is one million amperes, what is the resistance of the wire?

   0.002 ohms

5. What is the resistance of a lightbulb if a 120-volt potential difference produces a current of 0.8 A?

   150 ohms

Name_____

Ohm's Law Problems

Using Ohm's Law, solve each problem.

1. What is the current produced by a potential difference of 240 V through a resistance of 0.2 ohms?

   1,200 A

2. What resistance would produce a current of 120 A from a 6-volt battery?

   0.05 ohms

3. What voltage is necessary to produce a current of 200 A through a resistance of 1×10^{-3} ohms?

   0.2 V

4. What is the current produced by a 9-volt battery flowing through a resistance of 2×10^{-4} ohms?

   45,000 A

5. What is the potential difference if a resistance of 25 ohms produces a current of 250 A?

   6,250 V

Answer Key

Name_____

Calculating Power

P	=	V	$\times$	I
power (watts, W)	=	voltage (volts, V)	$\times$	current (amperes, A)

Solve each problem.

1. A 6-volt battery produces a current of 0.5 A. What is the power in the circuit?

   3 W

2. A 100-watt light bulb is operating on 1.2 A current. What is the voltage?

   83.3 W

3. A potential difference of 120 V is operating on a 500-watt microwave oven. What is the current being used?

   4.2 A

4. A lightbulb uses 0.625 A from a source of 120 V. How much power is used by the bulb?

   75 W

5. What voltage is necessary to run a 500-watt motor with a current of 200 A?

   2.5 V

© Carson-Dellosa • CD-104642   49

Name_____

Calculating Electrical Energy and Cost

Electrical energy is usually measured in units of kilowatt-hours (kWh). One kilowatt-hour is 1,000 watts of power for one hour of time.

Example: A coffee pot operates on 2 amps of current on a 110-volt circuit for 3 hours. Calculate the total kWh used.

1. Determine power. $P = V \times I$
   $= 110 \text{ V} \times 2 \text{ A}$
   $= 220 \text{ W}$

   $\text{kWh} = P \times \text{hours}$

   $\text{kWh} = \dfrac{V \times I \times \text{hours}}{1,000}$

2. Convert watts to kilowatts.
   $220 \text{ watts} \times \dfrac{1 \text{ kilowatt}}{1,000 \text{ watts}} = 0.22 \text{ kW}$

3. Multiply by the hours given in the problem.
   $0.22 \text{ kW} \times 3 \text{ hr} = 0.66 \text{ kWh}$

Solve each problem.

1. A microwave oven operates on 5 amps of current on a 110-volt circuit for one hour. Calculate the total kilowatt-hours used. _____**0.55 kWh**_____

2. How much would it cost to run the microwave in problem 1 if the cost of energy is $0.10 per kWh? _____**$0.06**_____

3. An electric stove operates on 20 amps of current on a 220-volt circuit for one hour. Calculate the total kilowatt-hours used. _____**4.4 kWh**_____

4. What is the cost of using the stove in problem 3 if the cost of energy if $0.10 per kWh? _____**$0.44**_____

5. A refrigerator operates on 15 amps of current on a 220-volt circuit for 18 hours per day. How many kilowatt hours are used per day? _____**59.4 kWh**_____

6. If the electric costs are 15¢ per kWh, how much does it cost to run the refrigerator in problem 5 per day? _____**$8.91**_____

7. The meter reading on June 1 was 84,502 kWh. On July 1, the meter read 87,498 kWh. If the cost of electricity in the area was 12¢ per kWh, what was the electric bill for the month of June? _____**$359.52**_____

8. A room was lighted with 3 100-watt bulbs for 5 hours per day. If the cost of electricity was 9¢ per kWh, how much would be saved per day by switching to 60-watt bulbs? _____**$0.05 (or 5.5¢)**_____

50   © Carson-Dellosa • CD-104642

Name_____

Series and Parallel Circuits

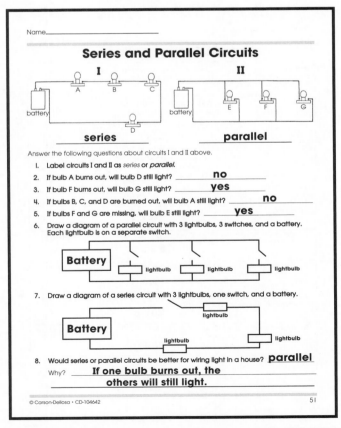

Answer the following questions about circuits I and II above.

1. Label circuits I and II as *series* or *parallel.*
2. If bulb A burns out, will bulb D still light? **no**
3. If bulb F burns out, will bulb G still light? _____ **yes**
4. If bulbs B, C, and D are burned out, will bulb A still light? _____ **no**
5. If bulbs F and G are missing, will bulb E still light? _____ **yes**
6. Draw a diagram of a parallel circuit with 3 lightbulbs, 3 switches, and a battery. Each lightbulb is on a separate switch.

7. Draw a diagram of a series circuit with 3 lightbulbs, one switch, and a battery.

8. Would series or parallel circuits be better for wiring light in a house? **parallel**
   Why? **If one bulb burns out, the others will still light.**

© Carson-Dellosa • CD-104642   51

Name_____

An Electric Motor

Label the following parts of the electric motor shown. List the function or purpose of each part.

horseshoe electromagnet (or permanent magnet) **produces a magnetic field so wire loop will rotate**

armature **carries current and converts electrical power to mechanical power**

commutator **switches direction of current flow so that poles of magnet are reversed**

brushes (+ and –) **supply current to the commutator**

field coil **carries current and converts electrical power to mechanical power**

current source **supplies current to coil so it becomes a magnet**

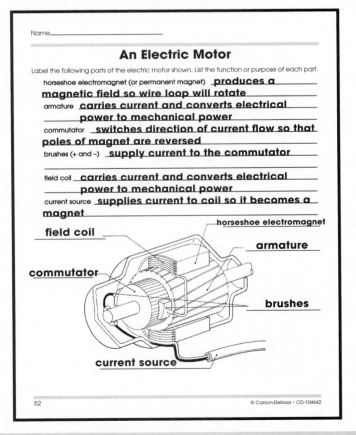

52   © Carson-Dellosa • CD-104642

© Carson-Dellosa • CD-104642

115

Answer Key

Name_____

An Electric Generator

Label the parts of an alternating current and a direct current generator. List the function or purpose of each part.

wire coils **create an electric field which interacts with the magnet**

brushes **conduct currents from slip rings to wires**

slip rings (ac only) **conduct current from armature to brushes**

commutator (dc only) **changes ac current to dc current**

armature **carries current and converts electrical power to mechanical power**

magnet **provides magnetic fields through which armature is rotated**

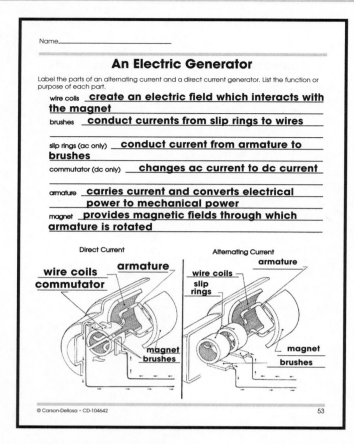

© Carson-Dellosa • CD-104642   53

Name_____

Transformers

Determine the voltage and current in each transformer.

Step-Up Transformer

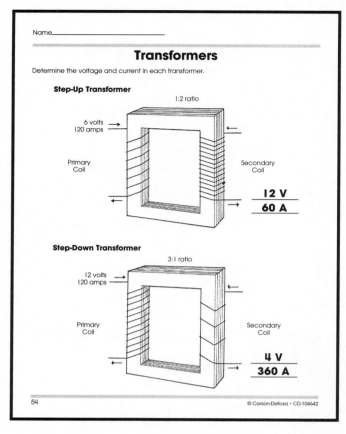

12 V
60 A

Step-Down Transformer

4 V
360 A

54   © Carson-Dellosa • CD-104642

Name_____

Electricity Crossword

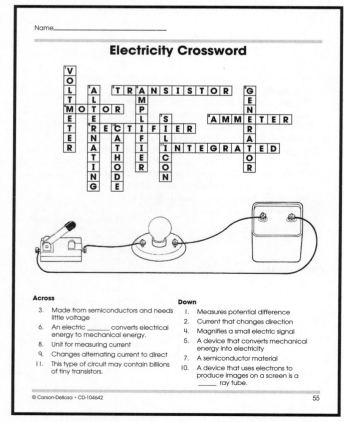

Across

3. Made from semiconductors and needs little voltage
6. An electric _____ converts electrical energy to mechanical energy.
8. Unit for measuring current
9. Changes alternating current to direct
11. This type of circuit may contain billions of tiny transistors.

Down

1. Measures potential difference
2. Current that changes direction
4. Magnifies a small electric signal
5. A device that converts mechanical energy into electricity
7. A semiconductor material
10. A device that uses electrons to produce images on a screen is a _____ ray tube.

© Carson-Dellosa • CD-104642   55

Name_____

Half-Life Calculations

Half-life is the time required for one-half of radioactive nuclei to decay (change to another element). It is possible to calculate the amount of a radioactive element that will be left if we know its half-life.

Example: The half-life of Po-214 is 0.001 second. How much of a 10-g sample will be left after 0.003 seconds?
Calculate the number of half-lives:

$$0.003 \text{ seconds} \times \frac{1 \text{ half-life}}{0.001 \text{ second}} = 3 \text{ half-lives}$$

After 0 half-lives, 10 g are left.
After 1 half-life, 5 g are left.
After 2 half-lives, 2.5 g are left.
After 3 half-lives, 1.25 g are left.

Solve each problem.

1. The half-life of radon-222 is 3.8 days. How much of a 100-g sample is left after 15.2 days?
   6.25 g

2. Carbon-14 has a half-life of 5,730 years. If a sample contains 70 mg originally, how much is left after 17,190 years?
   8.75 g

3. How much of a 500-g sample of potassium-42 is left after 62 hours? The half-life of K-42 is 12.4 hours.
   15.6 g

4. The half-life of cobalt-60 is 5.26 years. If 50 g are left after 15.8 years, how many grams were in the original sample?
   401 g

5. The half-life of I-131 is 8.07 days. If 25 g are left after 40.35 days, how many grams were in the original sample?
   800 g

6. If 100 g of Au-198 decays to 6.25 g in 10.8 days, what is the half-life of Au-198?
   2.7 days

56   © Carson-Dellosa • CD-104642

Answer Key

Name

A Nuclear Reactor

Label the parts of a nuclear reactor. List the function or purpose of each part.

control rods control the rate of the nuclear reaction by absorbing neutrons

reaction chamber contains the fuel; site for reactions

moderator slows down neutrons to allow them to be captured by the nuclei of the fuel

coolant absorbs thermal energy; regulates reactor temperature

shield protects reactor, surroundings, and humans from radiation

turbine generator produces electricity from movement of rotating blades

fuel fissionable material (U-235, U-238, Pu-239, U-233)

transformer changes voltage of electricity produced

heat exchanger transfers heat from reaction chamber

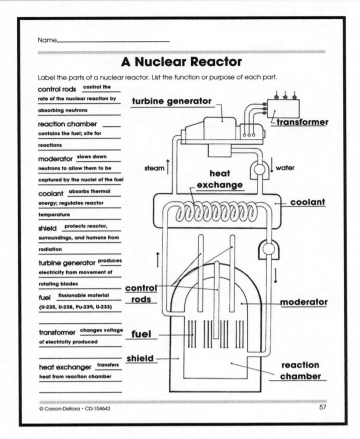

© Carson-Dellosa • CD-104642   57

Fuel Alternatives Crossword

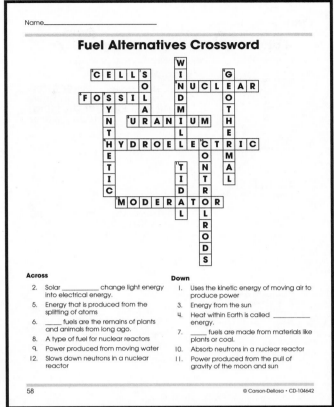

Across

2. Solar _____ change light energy into electrical energy.
5. Energy that is produced from the splitting of atoms
6. _____ fuels are the remains of plants and animals from long ago.
8. A type of fuel for nuclear reactors
9. Power produced from moving water
12. Slows down neutrons in a nuclear reactor

Down

1. Uses the kinetic energy of moving air to produce power
3. Energy from the sun
4. Heat within Earth is called _____ energy.
7. _____ fuels are made from materials like plants or coal.
10. Absorb neutrons in a nuclear reactor
11. Power produced from the pull of gravity of the moon and sun

58   © Carson-Dellosa • CD-104642

Substances and Mixtures

A **substance** is matter for which a chemical formula can be written. Elements and compounds are substances. **Mixtures** can be in any proportion, and the parts are not chemically bonded.

Classify each item as a mixture or substance by writing *M* or *S* in the space provided.

1. sodium — **S**
2. water — **S**
3. soil — **M**
4. coffee — **M**
5. oxygen — **S**
6. alcohol — **S**
7. carbon dioxide — **S**
8. cake batter — **M**
9. air — **M**
10. soup — **M**
11. iron — **S**
12. salt water — **M**
13. ice cream — **M**
14. nitrogen — **S**
15. eggs — **M**
16. blood — **M**
17. table salt — **S**
18. nail polish — **M**
19. milk — **M**
20. cola — **M**

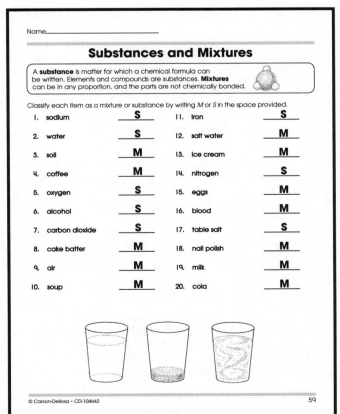

© Carson-Dellosa • CD-104642   59

Homogeneous vs. Heterogeneous Matter

Classify each substance or mixture as either homogeneous or heterogeneous. Place a check in the correct column.

	Homogeneous	Heterogeneous
1. flat soda pop	✓	
2. cherry vanilla ice cream		✓
3. salad dressing		✓
4. sugar	✓	
5. soil		✓
6. aluminum foil	✓	
7. black coffee	✓	
8. sugar water	✓	
9. city air		✓
10. paint		✓
11. alcohol	✓	
12. iron	✓	
13. beach sand		✓
14. pure air	✓	
15. spaghetti sauce		✓

60   © Carson-Dellosa • CD-104642

Answer Key

Name_____

Solutions, Colloids, and Suspensions

Label each mixture as a *solution*, *colloid*, or *suspension*. Then, give an example of each.

Examples will vary.

1. large particles, settles out on standing

   Kind of mixture: **suspension**
   Example: **chocolate milk, oil and vinegar dressing, muddy water**

2. medium-sized particles, does not settle out on standing, scatters light

   Kind of mixture: **colloid**
   Example: **fog, smoke, milk, whipped cream, paint, marshmallows**

3. very small particles, does not settle out on standing

   Kind of mixture: **solution**
   Example: **salt water, soda, vinegar, 3% hydrogen peroxide**

Name_____

Physical vs. Chemical Properties

A **physical property** is observed with the senses and can be determined without changing the indentity of the object. For example, color, shape, mass, length, density, specific heat, and odor are all examples of physical properties.

A **chemical property** indicates how a substance reacts with something else. The original substance is fundamentally changed in observing a chemical property. For example, the ability of iron to rust is a chemical property. The iron has reacted with oxygen, and the original iron metal is changed. It now exists as iron oxide, a different substance.

Classify each property as either chemical or physical by placing a check mark in the appropriate column.

		Physical Property	Chemical Property
1.	red color	✓	
2.	density	✓	
3.	flammability		✓
4.	solubility	✓	
5.	reacts with acid to form hydrogen		✓
6.	supports combustion		✓
7.	bitter taste	✓	
8.	melting point	✓	
9.	reacts with water to form a gas		✓
10.	reacts with a base to form water		✓
11.	hardness	✓	
12.	boiling point	✓	
13.	can neutralize a base		✓
14.	luster	✓	
15.	odor	✓	

Name_____

Physical vs. Chemical Changes

In a **physical change**, the original substance still exists; it only changes in form. In a **chemical change**, a new substance is produced. Energy changes always accompany chemical changes.

Classify each as a *physical* or *chemical* change.

1. Sodium hydroxide dissolves in water. **physical**

2. Hydrochloric acid reacts with potassium hydroxide to produce a salt, water, and heat. **chemical**

3. A pellet of sodium is sliced in two. **physical**

4. Water is heated and changed to steam. **physical**

5. Potassium chlorate decomposes to potassium chloride and oxygen gas. **chemical**

6. Iron rusts. **chemical**

7. Ice melts. **physical**

8. Acid on limestone produces carbon dioxide gas. **chemical**

9. Milk sours. **chemical**

10. Wood rots. **chemical**

Name_____

Separation of Mixtures

Taking advantage of various physical and chemical properties, describe how you would separate the following mixtures into their components.

1. sand and water **Filter the sand out or evaporate the water.**

2. sugar and water **Evaporate the water.**

3. oil and water **Allow them to separate due to their different densities, then skim or siphon the oil off.**

4. sand and gravel **Use a sieve to strain out the particles of a larger size.**

5. a mixture of heptane (boiling point 98°C) and heptanol (boiling point 176°C) **Heat it to 98°C, allowing the heptane to boil off, but keep it contained. The heptanol will remain in liquid form.**

6. a mixture of iodine solid and sodium chloride (Hint: iodine is not soluble in water.) **Mix with water to dissolve the sodium chloride. Then, filter out the iodine or evaporate the sodium chloride.**

7. a mixture of lead and aluminum pellets **Separate them by hand based on appearance. Or, shake them in water and allow them to settle in different layers based on their densities.**

8. a mixture of salt and iron filings **Use a magnet to separate out the iron fillings.**

Answer Key

States of Matter Crossword

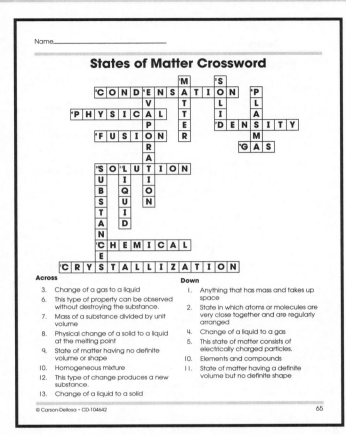

Across

3. Change of a gas to a liquid
6. This type of property can be observed without destroying the substance.
7. Mass of a substance divided by unit volume
8. Physical change of a solid to a liquid at the melting point
9. State of matter having no definite volume or shape
10. Homogeneous mixture
12. This type of change produces a new substance.
13. Change of a liquid to a solid

Down

1. Anything that has mass and takes up space
2. State in which atoms or molecules are very close together and are regularly arranged
4. Change of a liquid to a gas
5. This state of matter consists of electrically charged particles.
10. Elements and compounds
11. State of matter having a definite volume but no definite shape

65

Elements and Their Symbols

Identify the symbol for each element.

1. oxygen __O__
2. hydrogen __H__
3. chlorine __Cl__
4. sodium __Na__
5. fluorine __F__
6. carbon __C__
7. helium __He__
8. nitrogen __N__
9. copper __Cu__
10. sulfur __S__
11. magnesium __Mg__
12. manganese __Mn__
13. neon __Ne__
14. bromine __Br__
15. phosphorus __P__
16. silver __Ag__
17. lead __Pb__
18. iron __Fe__
19. calcium __Ca__
20. potassium __K__

Identify the name of the element that corresponds to each symbol.

21. Cu __copper__
22. K __potassium__
23. C __carbon__
24. Au __gold__
25. Zn __zinc__
26. Pb __lead__
27. Fe __iron__
28. Na __sodium__
29. S __sulfur__
30. Al __aluminum__
31. Ca __calcium__
32. Ag __silver__
33. P __phosphorus__
34. O __oxygen__
35. I __iodine__
36. Sn __tin__
37. H __hydrogen__
38. F __flourine__
39. NI __nickel__
40. Hg __mercury__

66

Elements and Minerals Crossword

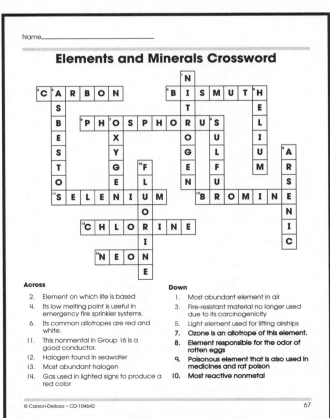

Across

2. Element on which life is based
4. Its low melting point is useful in emergency fire sprinkler systems.
6. Its common allotropes are red and white.
11. This nonmetal in Group 16 is a good conductor.
12. Halogen found in seawater
13. Most abundant halogen
14. Gas used in lighted signs to produce a red color

Down

1. Most abundant element in air
3. Fire-resistant material no longer used due to its carcinogenicity
5. Light element used for lifting airships
7. Ozone is an allotrope of this element.
8. Element responsible for the odor of rotten eggs
9. Poisonous element that is also used in medicines and rat poison
10. Most reactive nonmetal

67

Parts of an Atom

An atom is made up of protons and neutrons, which are in the nucleus, and electrons, which are in the electron cloud surrounding the atom.

The **atomic number** equals the number of protons. The electrons in a neutral atom equal the number of protons. The mass number equals the sum of the protons and neutrons.

The **charge** indicates the number of electrons that have been lost or gained. A positive charge indicates the number of electrons (which are negatively charged) lost. A negative charge indicates the number of electrons gained. This structure can be written as part of a chemical symbol.

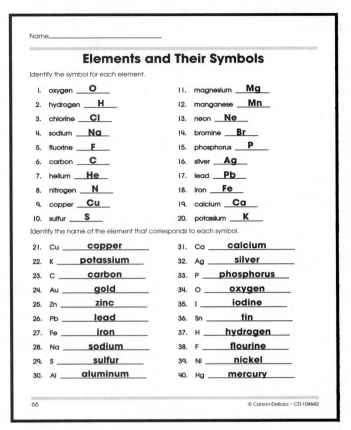

Complete the chart.

Element/ Ion	Atomic Number	Mass Number	Charge	Protons	Neutrons	Electrons
$^{24}_{12}Mg$	12	24	0	12	12	12
$^{39}_{19}K$	19	39	0	19	20	19
$^{23}_{11}Na^+$	11	23	+1	11	12	10
$^{19}_{9}F^-$	9	19	−1	9	10	10
$^{27}_{13}Al^{3+}$	13	27	+3	13	14	10
$^{1}_{1}H$	1	1	0	1	0	1
$^{24}Mg^{2+}$	12	24	+2	12	12	10
Ag	47	108	0	47	61	47
S^{2-}	16	32	−2	16	16	18
$^{2}_{1}H$	1	2	0	1	1	1
$^{35}Cl^-$	17	35	−1	17	18	18
Be^{2+}	4	9	+2	4	5	2

68

Answer Key

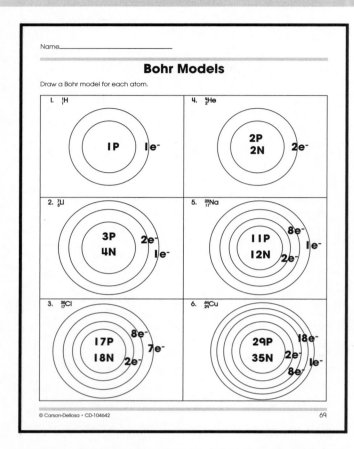

Bohr Models

Draw a Bohr model for each atom.

1. $^{1}_{1}H$ 1P 1e⁻	4. $^{4}_{2}He$ 2P 2N 2e⁻
2. $^{7}_{3}Li$ 3P 4N 2e⁻ 1e⁻	5. $^{23}_{11}Na$ 11P 12N 8e⁻ 1e⁻ 2e⁻
3. $^{35}_{17}Cl$ 17P 18N 8e⁻ 7e⁻ 2e⁻	6. $^{64}_{29}Cu$ 29P 35N 18e⁻ 2e⁻ 1e⁻ 8e⁻

Properties of Metals and Nonmetals

For each physical or chemical property, put a check in the appropriate column if it applies to a metal or a nonmetal.

Property	Metal	Nonmetal
1. malleable	✓	
2. lustrous	✓	
3. gaseous at room temperature		✓
4. forms negative ions		✓
5. metallic bonding	✓	
6. more than 4 valence electrons		✓
7. conducts electricity in a solid state	✓	
8. ductile	✓	
9. brittle		✓
10. only forms positive ions	✓	
11. nonconductor		✓
12. covalent bonding		✓
13. can have both positive and negative oxidation numbers		✓
14. gives away electrons in chemical reactions	✓	
15. prefers to receive electrons in chemical reactions		✓

Activity of the Elements

Since metals prefer to give away electrons during chemical bonding, the most active metals are closest to francium, which is a large atom with low ionization energy and electronegativity. Nonmetals prefer to pull in electrons, so the most active nonmetals are closest to fluorine, which has a high ionization energy and electronegativity. The noble gases (Group 18) are considered inactive since they already have a stable octet of electrons in their outer shell.

Referring to a periodic table, circle the member of each pair of elements which is most chemically active.

1. Li and (Na)
2. Cl₂ and (F₂)
3. (N₂) and N
4. (Rb) and Ca
5. Ti and (Ca)
6. (K) and Mg
7. (O₂) and S
8. I₂ and (Br₂)
9. (Na) and Zn
10. P and (S)
11. N₂ and (O₂)
12. (Cl₂) and Ar
13. Ba and (Fr)
14. (Rb) and Cu
15. (Be) and Cr

16. (Cl₂) and Br₂
17. Xe and (I₂)
18. Fe and (Ra)
19. (Sr) and Mn
20. (K) and Na
21. Au and (Mg)
22. (S) and Rn
23. (Li) and Be
24. Se and (Br₂)
25. I₂ and (F₂)
26. (Rb) and Sr
27. Ba and (Ra)
28. (Na) and Mg
29. Te and (I₂)
30. (Ca) and Rn

Periodic Table Puzzle

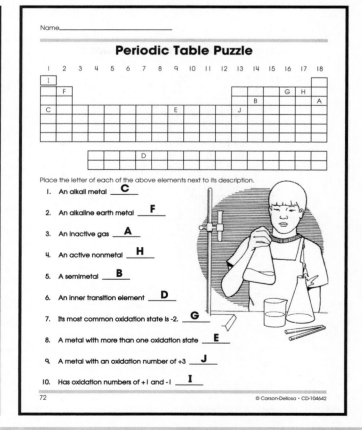

| 1 | 2 | 3 | 4 | 5 | 6 | 7 | 8 | 9 | 10 | 11 | 12 | 13 | 14 | 15 | 16 | 17 | 18 |

(periodic table grid with letters: I, F, G, H, B, A, C, E, J, D)

Place the letter of each of the above elements next to its description.

1. An alkali metal ___C___
2. An alkaline earth metal ___F___
3. An inactive gas ___A___
4. An active nonmetal ___H___
5. A semimetal ___B___
6. An inner transition element ___D___
7. Its most common oxidation state is -2. ___G___
8. A metal with more than one oxidation state ___E___
9. A metal with an oxidation number of +3 ___J___
10. Has oxidation numbers of +1 and -1 ___I___

Answer Key

Name_____

Periodic Table Crossword

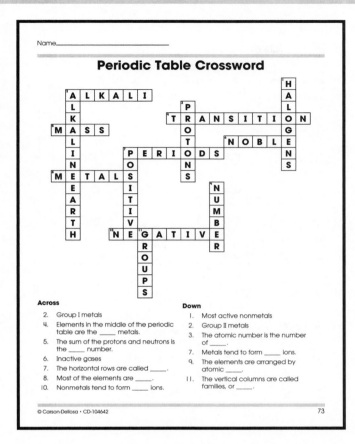

Across

2. Group I metals
4. Elements in the middle of the periodic table are the _____ metals.
5. The sum of the protons and neutrons is the _____ number.
6. Inactive gases
7. The horizontal rows are called _____.
8. Most of the elements are _____.
10. Nonmetals tend to form _____ ions.

Down

1. Most active nonmetals
2. Group II metals
3. The atomic number is the number of _____.
7. Metals tend to form _____ ions.
9. The elements are arranged by atomic _____.
11. The vertical columns are called families, or _____.

73

Name_____

Types of Chemical Bonds

Classify the following compounds as *ionic* (metal and nonmetal), *covalent* (nonmetal and nonmetal), or *both* (compound containing a polyatomic ion).

1. $CaCl_2$ — **ionic**
2. CO_2 — **covalent**
3. H_2O — **covalent**
4. $BaSO_4$ — **both**
5. K_2O — **ionic**
6. NaF — **ionic**
7. Na_2CO_3 — **both**
8. CH_4 — **covalent**
9. SO_3 — **covalent**
10. $LiBr$ — **ionic**

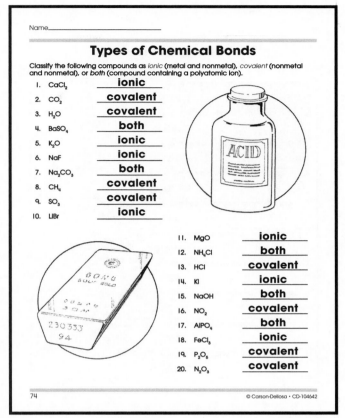

11. MgO — **ionic**
12. NH_4Cl — **both**
13. HCl — **covalent**
14. KI — **ionic**
15. $NaOH$ — **both**
16. NO_2 — **covalent**
17. $AlPO_4$ — **both**
18. $FeCl_3$ — **ionic**
19. P_2O_5 — **covalent**
20. N_2O_3 — **covalent**

74

Name_____

Number of Atoms in a Formula

Determine the number of atoms in each chemical formula.

1. $NaCl$ — **2**
2. H_2SO_4 — **7**
3. KNO_3 — **5**
4. $CaCl_2$ — **3**
5. C_2H_6 — **8**
6. $Ba(OH)_2$ — **5**
7. NH_4Br — **6**
8. $Ca_3(PO_4)_2$ — **13**
9. $Al_2(SO_4)_3$ — **17**
10. $Mg(NO_3)_2$ — **9**

11. $Cu(NO_3)_2$ — **9**
12. $KMnO_4$ — **6**
13. H_2O_2 — **4**
14. H_3PO_4 — **8**
15. $(NH_4)_3PO_4$ — **20**
16. Fe_2O_3 — **5**
17. $NaC_2H_3O_2$ — **8**
18. $Mg(C_2H_3O_2)_2$ — **15**
19. Hg_2Cl_2 — **4**
20. K_2SO_3 — **6**

75

Name_____

Gram Formula Mass

Determine the gram formula mass of each compound. Round to the nearest whole number.

1. $NaCl$ — **58 g**
2. H_2SO_4 — **98 g**
3. KNO_3 — **101 g**
4. $CaCl_2$ — **110 g**
5. C_2H_6 — **30 g**
6. $Ba(OH)_2$ — **171 g**
7. NH_4Br — **98 g**
8. $Ca_3(PO_4)_2$ — **310 g**
9. $Al_2(SO_4)_3$ — **342 g**
10. $Mg(NO_3)_2$ — **148 g**

11. $Cu(NO_3)_2$ — **188 g**
12. $KMnO_4$ — **158 g**
13. H_2O_2 — **34 g**
14. H_3PO_4 — **98 g**
15. $(NH_4)_3PO_4$ — **149 g**
16. Fe_2O_3 — **160 g**
17. $NaC_2H_3O_2$ — **82 g**
18. $Mg(C_2H_3O_2)_2$ — **142 g**
19. Hg_2Cl_2 — **472 g**
20. K_2SO_3 — **158 g**

76

Answer Key

Percentage Composition

Solve each problem. Round to the nearest whole number.

1. What is the percentage of carbon in CO_2?

   27%

2. How many grams of carbon are in 25 g of CO_2?

   6.75 g

3. What is the percentage of sodium in NaCl?

   39%

4. How many grams of sodium are in 75 g of NaCl?

   29.25 g

5. What is the percentage of oxygen in $KClO_3$?

   39%

6. How many grams of oxygen can be obtained from 5.00 g of $KClO_3$?

   1.95 g

7. What is the percentage of silver in $AgNO_3$?

   63%

8. How many grams of silver can be recovered from 125 g of $AgNO_3$?

   78.75 g

9. What is the percentage of gold in $AuCl_3$?

   65%

10. How many grams of gold can be recovered from 35.0 g of $AuCl_3$?

    22.75 g

Writing Binary Formulas

Write the formula for the compounds formed from each ion.

1. Na^+, Cl^- — **NaCl**
2. Ba^{+2}, F^- — **BaF_2**
3. K^+, S^{-2} — **K_2S**
4. Li^+, Br^- — **LiBr**
5. Al^{+3}, I^- — **AlI_3**
6. Zn^{+2}, S^{-2} — **ZnS**
7. Ag^+, O^{-2} — **Ag_2O**
8. Mg^{+2}, P^{-3} — **Mg_3P_2**
9. Ni^{+2}, O^{-2} — **NiO**
10. Ni^{+3}, O^{-2} — **Ni_2O_3**
11. Fe^{+2}, O^{-2} — **FeO**
12. Fe^{+3}, O^{-2} — **Fe_2O_3**
13. Cr^{+2}, S^{-2} — **CrS**
14. Cr^{+3}, S^{-2} — **Cr_2S_3**
15. Cu^+, Cl^- — **CuCl**
16. Cu^{+2}, Cl^- — **$CuCl_2$**
17. Pb^{+2}, O^{-2} — **PbO**
18. Pb^{+4}, O^{-2} — **PbO_2**
19. Mn^{+2}, Br^- — **$MnBr_2$**
20. Mn^{+4}, Br^- — **$MnBr_4$**

Naming Binary Compounds (Ionic)

Name each ionic compound, using Roman numerals where necessary.

1. $BaCl_2$ — **barium chloride**
2. NaF — **sodium fluoride**
3. Ag_2O — **silver oxide**
4. CuBr — **copper(I) bromide**
5. $CuBr_2$ — **copper(II) bromide**
6. FeO — **iron(II) oxide**
7. Fe_2O_3 — **iron(III) oxide**
8. MgS — **magnesium sulfide**
9. Al_2O_3 — **aluminum oxide**
10. CaI_2 — **calcium iodide**
11. K_2S — **potassium sulfide**
12. $CrCl_2$ — **chromium(II) chloride**
13. $CrCl_3$ — **chromium(III) chloride**
14. CaO — **calcium oxide**
15. Ba_3P_2 — **barium phosphide**
16. Hg_2I_2 — **mercury(I) iodide**
17. Na_2O — **sodium oxide**
18. BeS — **beryllium sulfide**
19. MnO — **manganese(II) oxide**
20. Mn_2O_3 — **manganese(III) oxide**

Naming Binary Compounds (Covalent)

Name each compound using the prefix method.

1. CO — **carbon monoxide**
2. CO_2 — **carbon dioxide**
3. SO_2 — **sulfur dioxide**
4. NO_2 — **nitrogen dioxide**
5. N_2O — **dinitrogen monoxide**
6. SO_3 — **sulfur trioxide**
7. CCl_4 — **carbon tetrachloride**
8. NO — **nitrogen monoxide**
9. N_2O_5 — **dinitrogen pentoxide**
10. P_2O_5 — **diphosphorous pentoxide**
11. N_2O_4 — **dinitrogen tetroxide**
12. CS_2 — **carbon disulfide**
13. OF_2 — **oxygen difluoride**
14. PCl_3 — **phosphorous trichloride**
15. PBr_5 — **phosphorus pentabromide**

Answer Key

Name_____

Formulas (with Polyatomic Ions)

Matching the horizontal and vertical axes, write the formulas of the compounds with the following combination of ions. The first row is done for you.

	OH^-	NO_3^-	CO_3^{2-}	SO_4^{2-}	PO_4^{3-}
H^+	HOH (H_2O)	HNO_3	H_2CO_3	H_2SO_4	H_3PO_4
Na^+	$NaOH$	$NaNO_3$	Na_2CO_3	Na_2SO_4	Na_3PO_4
Mg^{2+}	$Mg(OH)_2$	$Mg(NO_3)_2$	$MgCO_3$	$MgSO_4$	$Mg_3(PO_4)_2$
NH_4^+	NH_4OH	NH_4NO_3	$(NH_4)_2CO_3$	$(NH_4)_2SO_4$	$(NH_4)_3PO_4$
Ca^{2+}	$Ca(OH)_2$	$Ca(NO_3)_2$	$CaCO_3$	$CaSO_4$	$Ca_3(PO_4)_2$
K^+	KOH	KNO_3	K_2CO_3	K_2SO_4	K_3PO_4
Al^{3+}	$Al(OH)_3$	$Al(NO_3)_3$	$Al_2(CO_3)_3$	$Al_2(SO_4)_3$	$AlPO_4$
Pb^{4+}	$Pb(OH)_4$	$Pb(NO_3)_4$	$Pb(CO_3)_2$	$Pb(SO_4)_2$	$Pb_3(PO_4)_4$

81

Name_____

Naming of Non-Binary Compounds

An ionic compound that contains more than two elements must contain a polyatomic ion.

Name each compound.

1. $NaNO_3$ — sodium nitrate
2. $Ca(OH)_2$ — calcium hydroxide
3. K_2CO_3 — potassium carbonate
4. NH_4Cl — ammonium chloride
5. $MgSO_4$ — magnesium sulfate
6. $AlPO_4$ — aluminum phosphate
7. $(NH_4)_2SO_4$ — ammonium sulfate
8. Na_3PO_4 — trisodium phosphate
9. $CuSO_4$ — copper(II) sulfate
10. NH_4OH — ammonium hydroxide
11. Li_2SO_3 — lithium sulfite
12. $Mg(NO_3)_2$ — magnesium nitrate
13. $Al(OH)_3$ — aluminum hydroxide
14. $(NH_4)_3PO_4$ — ammonium phosphate
15. KOH — potassium hydroxide
16. $Ca(NO_3)_2$ — calcium nitrate
17. K_2SO_4 — potassium sulfate
18. $Pb(OH)_2$ — lead(II) hydroxide
19. Na_2O_2 — sodium peroxide
20. $CuCO_3$ — copper(II) carbonate

82

Name_____

Naming Compounds (Mixed)

Name each compound.

1. $NaCl$ — sodium chloride
2. MnS — manganese sulfide
3. K_2O — potassium oxide
4. $CuBr_2$ — copper(II) bromide
5. $CuBr$ — copper(I) bromide
6. CO_2 — carbon dioxide
7. $PbSO_4$ — lead(II) sulfate
8. Li_2CO_3 — lithium carbonate
9. Na_2CO_3 — sodium carbonate
10. NO_2 — nitrogen dioxide
11. N_2O_4 — dinitrogen tetroxide
12. $Ca(OH)_2$ — calcium hydroxide
13. NH_4Cl — ammonium chloride
14. SO_3 — sulfur trioxide
15. $AlPO_4$ — aluminum phosphate
16. CCl_4 — carbon tetrachloride
17. CaS — calcium sulfide
18. NH_3 — ammonia
19. MgI_2 — magnesium iodide
20. K_3PO_4 — potassium phosphate

83

Name_____

Writing Formulas from Names

Write the formula for each compound.

1. carbon monoxide — CO
2. sodium chloride — $NaCl$
3. carbon tetrachloride — CCl_4
4. magnesium bromide — $MgBr_2$
5. aluminum iodide — AlI_3
6. hydrogen hydroxide — HOH
7. iron(II) fluoride — FeF_2
8. carbon dioxide — CO_2
9. sodium carbonate — Na_2CO_3
10. ammonium sulfide — $(NH_4)_2S$
11. iron(II) oxide — FeO
12. iron(III) oxide — Fe_2O_3
13. magnesium sulfate — $MgSO_4$
14. sodium phosphate — Na_3PO_4
15. dinitrogen pentoxide — N_2O_5
16. phosphorus trichloride — PCl_3
17. aluminum sulfite — $Al_2(SO_3)_3$
18. copper(I) carbonate — Cu_2CO_3
19. potassium hydrogen carbonate — $KHCO_3$
20. sulfur trioxide — SO_3

84

123

Answer Key

Name_____

Balancing Equations

Balance each chemical equation.

1. $CH_4 + 2O_2 \longrightarrow CO_2 + 2H_2O$

2. $2Na + I_2 \longrightarrow 2NaI$

3. $2N_2 + O_2 \longrightarrow 2N_2O$

4. $N_2 + 3H_2 \longrightarrow 2NH_3$

5. $2KI + Cl_2 \longrightarrow 2KCl + I_2$

6. $2HCl + Ca(OH)_2 \longrightarrow CaCl_2 + 2H_2O$

7. $2KClO_3 \longrightarrow 2KCl + 3O_2$

8. $K_3PO_4 + 3HCl \longrightarrow 3KCl + H_3PO_4$

9. $2S + 3O_2 \longrightarrow 2SO_3$

10. $2KI + Pb(NO_3)_2 \longrightarrow 2KNO_3 + PbI_2$

11. $3CaSO_4 + 2AlBr_3 \longrightarrow 3CaBr_2 + Al_2(SO_4)_3$

12. $2H_2O_2 \longrightarrow 2H_2O + O_2$

13. $2Na + 2H_2O \longrightarrow 2NaOH + H_2$

14. $2C_2H_6 + 7O_2 \longrightarrow 4CO_2 + 6H_2O$

15. $3Mg(NO_3)_2 + 2K_3PO_4 \longrightarrow Mg_3(PO_4)_2 + 6KNO_3$

Name_____

Word Equations

Write and balance each chemical equation.

1. Hydrogen plus oxygen yield water.
$2H_2 + O_2 \longrightarrow 2H_2O$

2. Nitrogen plus hydrogen yield ammonia.
$N_2 + 3H_2 \longrightarrow 2NH_3$

3. Aluminum bromide plus chlorine yield aluminum chloride and bromine.
$2AlBr_3 + 3Cl_2 \longrightarrow 2AlCl_3 + 3Br_2$

4. Hydrochloric acid plus sodium hydroxide yield sodium chloride plus water.
$HCl + NaOH \longrightarrow NaCl + H_2O$

5. Iron plus lead(II) sulfate react forming iron(II) sulfate plus lead.
$Fe + PbSO_4 \longrightarrow FeSO_4 + Pb$

6. Potassium chlorate, when heated, produces potassium chloride plus oxygen gas.
$2KClO_3 \longrightarrow 2KCl + 3O_2$

7. Sulfuric acid decomposes to form sulfur trioxide gas plus water.
$H_2SO_4 \longrightarrow SO_3 + H_2O$

8. Sodium oxide combines with water to make sodium hydroxide.
$Na_2O + H_2O \longrightarrow 2NaOH$

9. Potassium iodide reacts with bromine, forming potassium bromide plus iodine.
$2KI + Br_2 \longrightarrow 2KBr + I_2$

10. Sodium phosphate reacts with calcium nitrate to produce sodium nitrate plus calcium phosphate. $2Na_3PO_4 + 3Ca(NO_3)_2 \longrightarrow 6NaNO_3 + Ca_3(PO_4)_2$

11. Zinc reacts with iron(III) chloride yielding zinc chloride plus iron precipitate.
$3Zn + 2FeCl_3 \longrightarrow 3ZnCl_2 + 2Fe$

12. Ammonium carbonate and magnesium sulfate react to yield ammonium sulfate plus magnesium carbonate. $(NH_4)_2CO_3 + MgSO_4 \longrightarrow (NH_4)_2SO_4 + MgCO_3$

13. Phosphoric acid plus calcium hydroxide react, forming solid calcium phosphate plus water. $2H_3PO_4 + 2Ca(OH_2) \longrightarrow Ca_3(PO_4)_2 + 6H_2$

14. Aluminum plus oxygen gas form aluminum oxide under certain conditions.
$4Al + 3O_2 \longrightarrow 2Al_2O_3$

15. Nitrogen gas plus oxygen gas react and form dinitrogen pentoxide.
$2N_2 + 5O_2 \longrightarrow 2N_2O_5$

Name_____

Identifying Chemical Reactions

Identify each reaction as *synthesis, decomposition, single replacement,* or *double replacement*.

1. $2KClO_3 \longrightarrow 2KCl + 3O_2$ — **decomposition**

2. $HCl + NaOH \longrightarrow NaCl + H_2O$ — **double replacement**

3. $Mg + 2HCl \longrightarrow MgCl_2 + H_2$ — **single replacement**

4. $2H_2 + O_2 \longrightarrow 2H_2O$ — **synthesis**

5. $2Al + 3NiBr_2 \longrightarrow 2AlBr_3 + 3Ni$ — **single replacement**

6. $4Al + 3O_2 \longrightarrow 2Al_2O_3$ — **synthesis**

7. $2NaCl \longrightarrow 2Na + Cl_2$ — **decomposition**

8. $CaCl_2 + F_2 \longrightarrow CaF_2 + Cl_2$ — **single replacement**

9. $AgNO_3 + KCl \longrightarrow AgCl + KNO_3$ — **double replacement**

10. $N_2 + 3H_2 \longrightarrow 2NH_3$ — **synthesis**

11. $2H_2O_2 \longrightarrow 2H_2O + O_2$ — **decomposition**

12. $(NH_4)_2SO_4 + Ba(NO_3)_2 \longrightarrow BaSO_4 + 2NH_4NO_3$ — **double replacement**

13. $MgI_2 + Br_2 \longrightarrow MgBr_2 + I_2$ — **single replacement**

14. $SO_3 + H_2O \longrightarrow H_2SO_4$ — **synthesis**

15. $6KCl + Zn_3(PO_4)_2 \longrightarrow 3ZnCl_2 + 2K_3PO_4$ — **double replacement**

Name_____

Conservation of Mass

In chemical reactions, mass is neither gained nor lost. The total mass of all the reactants equals the total mass of all the products. Atoms are just rearranged into different compounds.

Using the idea of conservation of mass, solve each problem.

1. $2KClO_3 \longrightarrow 2KCl + 3O_2$
If 500 g of $KClO_3$ decompresses and produces 303 g of KCl, how many grams of O_2 are produced?
197 g

2. $N_2 + 3H_2 \longrightarrow 2NH_3$
How many grams of H_2 are needed to react with 100 g of N_2 to produce 121 g of NH_3?
21 g

3. $4Fe + 3O_2 \longrightarrow 2Fe_2O_3$
How many grams of oxygen are needed to react with 350 g of iron to produce 500 g of Fe_2O_3?
150 g

4. $CH_4 + 2O_2 \longrightarrow CO_2 + 2H_2O$
Sixteen g of CH_4 react with 64 g of O_2, producing 44 g of CO_2. How many grams of water are produced?
36 g

5. $CaCO_3 \longrightarrow CaO + CO_2$
How much CO_2 is produced from the decomposition of 200 g of $CaCO_3$ if 112 g of CaO are produced?
88 g

Answer Key

Name_____

Mass Relationships in Equations

A balanced equation can tell us the mass relationships involved in a chemical reaction.

Example: $2KClO_3 \longrightarrow 2KCl + 3O_2$

How many grams of KCl are produced if 244 g of $KClO_3$ decompose?

1 formula mass of $KClO_3$ = 122 g

1 formula mass of KCl = 74 g

$$244 \text{ g of } KClO_3 \times \frac{2(74 \text{ g}) \text{ KCl}}{2(122 \text{ g}) \text{ } KClO_3} = 148 \text{ g KCl}$$

coefficients from equation

Example: $N_2 + 3H_2 \longrightarrow 2NH_3$

How many grams of H_2 are needed to react with 56 g of N_2?

1 formula mass of N_2 = 28 g

1 formula mass of H_2 = 2 g

$$56 \text{ g } N_2 \times \frac{3(2 \text{ g}) H_2}{1(28 \text{ g}) N_2} = 12 \text{ g}$$

Solve each problem.

1. $2H_2O_2 \longrightarrow 2H_2O + O_2$
   How many grams of water are produced from the decomposition of 68 g of H_2O_2?
   36 g

2. How many grams of oxygen are produced in the above reaction?
   32 g

3. $2C_2H_6 + 7O_2 \longrightarrow 4CO_2 + 6H_2O$
   How many grams of oxygen are required to completely react with 120 g of C_2H_6?
   448 g

4. How many grams of CO_2 are produced in the above reaction?
   352 g

5. $2K_3PO_4 + 3MgCl_2 \longrightarrow Mg_3(PO_4)_2 + 6KCl$
   How much $MgCl_2$ is required to react exactly with 500 g of K_3PO_4?
   333 g

6. How much KCl will be produced in the above reaction?
   524 g

89

Name_____

Acid, Base, or Salt?

Identify each compound as an *acid*, a *base*, or a *salt*. Then, indicate whether each acid and base is *strong* or *weak*.

1.	HNO_3	acid	strong
2.	NaOH	base	strong
3.	$NaNO_3$	salt	
4.	HCl	acid	strong
5.	KCl	salt	
6.	$Ba(OH)_2$	base	strong
7.	KOH	base	strong
8.	H_2S	acid	weak
9.	$Al(NO_3)_3$	salt	
10.	H_2SO_4	acid	strong
11.	$CaCl_2$	salt	
12.	H_3PO_4	acid	weak
13.	Na_2SO_4	salt	
14.	$Mg(OH)_2$	base	strong
15.	H_2CO_3	acid	weak
16.	NH_4OH	base	weak
17.	NH_4Cl	salt	
18.	HBr	acid	strong
19.	$FeBr_3$	salt	
20.	HF	acid	weak

90

Name_____

pH

pH is a measure of the concentration of hydronium ions in a solution. It uses a scale ranging from 0 to 14, with 0 being the most acidic and 14 being the most basic.

Indicators are substances that change color at different pH levels. Phenolphthalein is colorless in an acid and a neutral solution, but pink in a base. Blue litmus changes to red in an acid, and remains blue in neutral and basic solutions. Red litmus remains red in acidic and neutral substances, but turns blue in bases.

Complete the chart.

pH	Acid , Base, or Neutral	Phenolphthalein	Blue Litmus	Red Litmus
2	acid	colorless	red	red
8	base	pink	blue	blue
4	acid	colorless	red	red
7	neutral	colorless	blue	red
13	base	pink	blue	blue
11	base	pink	blue	blue
5	acid	colorless	red	red
1	acid	colorless	red	red

91

Name_____

pH of Salt Solutions

A **salt** is formed from the reaction of an acid and a base.

A strong acid + a strong base $\longrightarrow$ neutral salt

A strong acid + a weak base $\longrightarrow$ acidic salt

A weak acid + a strong base $\longrightarrow$ basic salt

The salt of a weak acid and a weak base may be acidic, neutral, or basic, depending on the relative strengths of the acids and bases involved.

The strong acids are HI, HBr, HCl, HNO_3, H_2SO_4, and $HClO_4$. The strong bases are the Group I and Group II hydroxides. Most others are considered weak.

Complete the chart. The first row is done for you.

Salt	Parent Acid	Acid Strength	Parent Base	Base Strength	Type of Salt
KBr	HBr	strong	KOH	strong	neutral
$Fe(NO_3)_2$	HNO_3	strong	$Fe(OH)_2$	weak	acidic
NaF	HF	weak	NaOH	strong	basic
NH_4Cl	HCl	strong	NH_4OH	weak	acidic
$Ca(NO_3)_2$	HNO_3	strong	$Ca(OH)_2$	strong	neutral
Li_3PO_4	H_3PO_4	weak	LiOH	strong	basic
K_2SO_4	H_2SO_4	strong	KOH	strong	neutral
AlI_3	HI	strong	$Al(OH)_3$	weak	acidic
$MgCO_3$	H_2CO_3	weak	$Mg(OH)_2$	strong	basic
$Zn(ClO_4)_2$	$HClO_4$	strong	$Zn(OH)_2$	weak	acidic

92

Answer Key

Name

Conductors and Electrolytes

Pure metals are good conductors of electricity. **Electrolytes** are aqueous solutions that conduct electricity. Acids, bases, and salts (ionic compounds) are electrolytes. **Nonelectrolytes** are aqueous solutions that do not conduct electricity. The solutes used to form nonelectrolytes are covalently bonded.

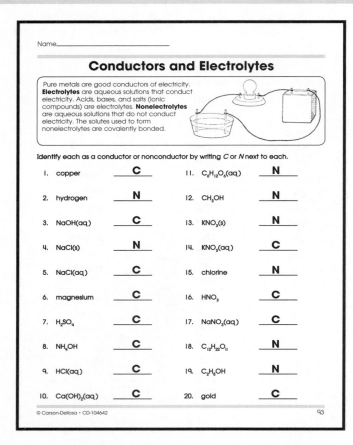

Identify each as a conductor or nonconductor by writing *C* or *N* next to each.

1. copper — **C**
2. hydrogen — **N**
3. NaOH(aq) — **C**
4. NaCl(s) — **N**
5. NaCl(aq) — **C**
6. magnesium — **C**
7. H_2SO_4 — **C**
8. NH_4OH — **C**
9. HCl(aq) — **C**
10. $Ca(OH)_2(aq)$ — **C**

11. $C_6H_{12}O_6(aq)$ — **N**
12. CH_3OH — **N**
13. $KNO_3(s)$ — **N**
14. $KNO_3(aq)$ — **C**
15. chlorine — **N**
16. HNO_3 — **C**
17. $NaNO_3(aq)$ — **C**
18. $C_{12}H_{22}O_{11}$ — **N**
19. C_2H_5OH — **N**
20. gold — **C**

Name

Effect of Dissolved Particles on Freezing and Boiling Points

The graph below shows a time/temperature graph for the heating of water. Directly on the graph, sketch the approximate curve that would result when

A. 5 g of sugar ($C_6H_{12}O_6$) are dissolved in the sample;
B. 5 g of NaCl are dissolved;
C. 10 g of NaCl are dissolved.

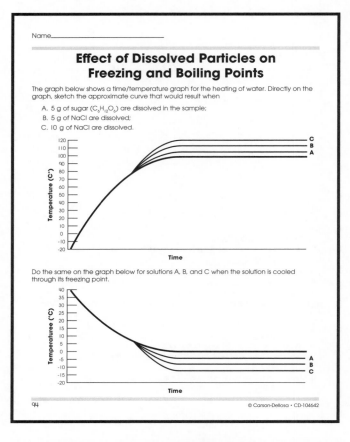

Do the same on the graph below for solutions A, B, and C when the solution is cooled through its freezing point.

Name

Concentration (Mass/Volume)

$$\text{concentration (in g/L)} = \frac{\text{mass of solute}}{\text{volume of solution}}$$

Solve each problem.

1. A sugar solution contains 26 g of sugar in 0.50 L of solution. What is the concentration?

   52 g/L

2. 45 grams of salt are dissolved in 0.10 L of solution. What is the concentration in g/L?

   450 g/L

3. A solution contains 25 g of sugar per L of solution. How many grams of sugar are in 1.5 L of solution?

   37.5 g

4. A solution contains 85 g of corn syrup per L of solution. How many grams of corn syrup are in 500 mL of solution?

   42.5 g

5. How many liters of salt solution would be needed to provide 30 g of salt if the concentration of the solution is 20 g/L?

   1.5 L

Name

Concentration (Percent by Volume)

$$\% \text{ volume} = \frac{V_{solute}}{V_{total}} \times 100\%$$

Solve each problem. Assume all volumes are additive.

1. To make 100 mL of solution, 25 mL of ethanol are added to water. Find the percent by volume of ethanol.

   25%

2. 50 mL of ethanol are added to 100 mL of water. What is the percent by volume of ethanol?

   50%

3. 3.0 L of antifreeze are added to 4.0 L of water. Find the percent by volume of antifreeze.

   75%

4. A popular fruit drink contains 5% by volume of fruit juice. How much fruit juice is in 500 mL of the fruit drink?

   25 mL

5. How much corn syrup should be added to water to make 200 mL of a 10% by-volume solution?

   20 mL

Answer Key

Answer Key

Isomers

Isomers have the same chemical formula but different structural formulas.

Match the structure with its isomer.

1. ___B___

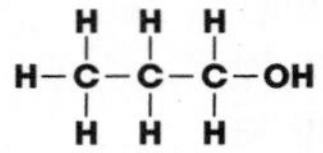

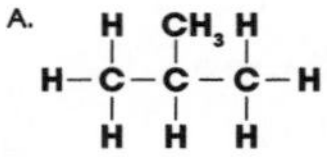

2. ___D___

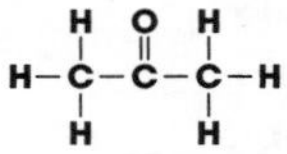

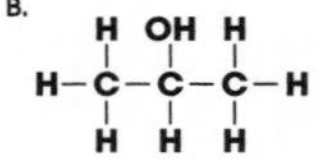

3. ___A___

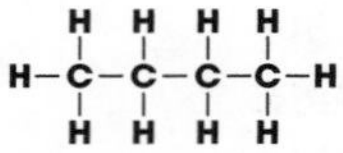

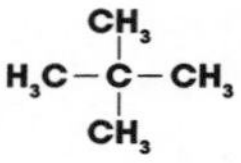

4. ___C___

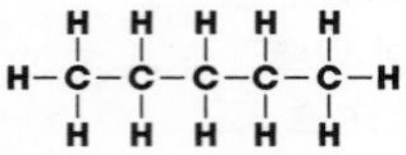

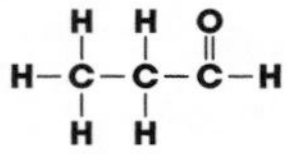

5. ___E___

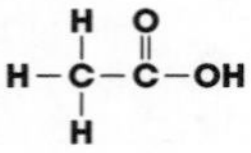

A.

B.

C.

D.

E.

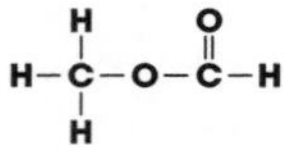

101